Skills Assessments, (

Table of Contents

Class Record Chart 2
Individual Student Chart 4

Unit 1: Reading

Reading Overall Assessment 5
Phonics
  Consonant Sounds 7
  Consonant Blends 8
  Long and Short Vowels 9
  Variant Vowels 10
Vocabulary
  Word Meaning 11
  Word Meaning in Context 12
  Words with Multiple Meanings 13
  Antonyms 14
  Synonyms 15
  Classifying 16
  Analogies 17
  Affixes and Compound Words 18
Reading Comprehension
  Facts 19
  Sequence 20
  Context 21
  Main Idea 22
  Conclusion 23
  Inference 24
  Fantasy 25
  Realistic Fiction 29
  Nonfiction 33

Unit 2: Language Arts

Language Arts Overall Assessment 37
Capitalization 39
Punctuation 41
Capitalization and Punctuation 43
Grammar and Usage
  Verbs 44
  Pronouns 45
  Using Words Correctly 46
  Sentence Parts 47
  Clear Sentences 48
Spelling* 49
Study Skills
  Reference Materials 52
  Parts of a Book 53
  ABC Order and Dictionary Skills 54
  Charts and Graphs 55
Writing Skills
  Personal Narrative and Information Paragraph 56
  Friendly Letter 57
  How-To Paragraph 58
  Descriptive Paragraph 59
  Persuasive Paragraph 60

Unit 3: Math

Math Overall Assessment 61
Number Concepts 63
Addition and Subtraction of Whole Numbers 65
Multiplication and Division of Whole Numbers 66
Mixed Operations with Whole Numbers 67
Geometry 68
Measurement 69
Fractions and Decimals 70
Statistics and Probability 71
Pre-Algebra: Patterns 72
Money 74
Time 75
Estimation 76
Problem Solving
  Whole Numbers 77
  Measurement and Geometry 79
  Fractions and Decimals 80

Unit 4: Science

Science Overall Assessment 81
Earth and Space Science 82
Life Science 84
Physical Science 86
Portfolio Assessment 88

Unit 5: Social Studies

Social Studies Overall Assessment 89
Reading Maps 92
Reading Time Lines 94

Answer Key 95

*PLEASE NOTE: Page 51 (Spelling) includes a list of 100 words that students should learn to spell. These are high-frequency words that are often misspelled. This list may be given to determine proficiency at the beginning of the year. A copy could be sent home for students to use as homework over an extended period of time.

Class Record Chart

Students	**Reading: Overall**	Consonant Sounds	Consonant Blends	Long and Short Vowels	Variant Vowels	Word Meaning	Word Meaning in Context	Words with Multiple Meanings	Antonyms	Synonyms	Classifying	Analogies	Affixes and Compound Words	Facts	Sequence	Context	Main Idea	Conclusion	Inference	Fantasy	Realistic Fiction	Nonfiction	**Language Arts: Overall**	Capitalization	Punctuation	Capitalization and Punctuation	Verbs	Pronouns	Using Words Correctly	Sentence Parts

Class Record Chart

Students	Clear Sentences	Spelling	Reference Materials	Parts of a Book	ABC Order & Dictionary Skills	Charts and Graphs	Personal Narrative/Info. Paragraph	Friendly Letter	How-To Paragraph	Descriptive Paragraph	Persuasive Paragraph	**Math: Overall**	Number Concepts	Addition and Subtraction	Multiplication and Division	Mixed Operations	Geometry	Measurement	Fractions and Decimals	Statistics and Probability	Pre-Algebra: Patterns	Money	Time	Estimation	Problem Solving: Whole Numbers	Problem Solving: Measurement and Geometry	Problem Solving: Fractions and Decimals	**Science: Overall**	Earth and Space Science	Life Science	Physical Science	**Social Studies: Overall**	Reading Maps	Reading Time Lines

Name ____________________

Individual Student Chart

	Test	Retest
Reading: Overall		
Consonant Sounds		
Consonant Blends		
Long and Short Vowels		
Variant Vowels		
Word Meaning		
Word Meaning in Context		
Words with Multiple Meanings		
Antonyms		
Synonyms		
Classifying		
Analogies		
Affixes and Compound Words		
Facts		
Sequence		
Context		
Main Idea		
Conclusion		
Inference		
Fantasy		
Realistic Fiction		
Nonfiction		
Language Arts: Overall		
Capitalization		
Punctuation		
Capitalization and Punctuation		
Verbs		
Pronouns		
Using Words Correctly		
Sentence Parts		
Clear Sentences		
Spelling		

	Test	Retest
Reference Materials		
Parts of a Book		
ABC Order & Dictionary Skills		
Charts and Graphs		
Personal Narrative; Information Paragraph		
Friendly Letter		
How-to Paragraph		
Descriptive Paragraph		
Persuasive Paragraph		
Math: Overall		
Number Concepts		
Addition and Subtraction of Whole Numbers		
Multiplication and Division of Whole Numbers		
Mixed Operations with Whole Numbers		
Geometry		
Measurement		
Fractions and Decimals		
Statistics and Probability		
Pre-Algebra: Patterns		
Money		
Time		
Estimation		
Problem Solving: Whole Numbers		
Problem Solving: Measurement and Geometry		
Problem Solving: Fractions and Decimals		
Science: Overall		
Earth and Space Science		
Life Science		
Physical Science		
Social Studies: Overall		
Reading Maps		
Reading Time Lines		

Name ______________________________ Date ______________

Reading Overall Assessment

1.  Write the letters that stand for the first, middle, and last sounds.

______i______e______

2. Write the answer. Is it a stamp, scale, or star?

____

3. Write the letters that stand for the missing vowels.

f______v______

Directions Darken the circle for the correct answer.

4. Jill can play the ___.

- Ⓐ dress
- Ⓑ drums
- Ⓒ book
- Ⓓ candy

5. Choose an antonym for pale.

- Ⓐ pail
- Ⓑ light
- Ⓒ dark
- Ⓓ bucket

6. Choose the one that does not belong.

- Ⓐ uncle
- Ⓑ sister
- Ⓒ mother
- Ⓓ aunt

7. Over is to under as ___ is to far.

- Ⓐ up
- Ⓑ long
- Ⓒ near
- Ⓓ trip

8. Choose the base word for unhappily.

- Ⓐ unhappi
- Ⓑ happily
- Ⓒ happi
- Ⓓ happy

Go on to the next page.

Name ______________________ Date ______________

Reading Overall Assessment, p. 2

Directions Read the paragraph. Darken the circle for the correct answer.

It was the last inning of the game, and there were two outs. Kate's team was one run behind with the tying run on base. Kate knew she was a pretty good player, but even so, she was scared. She swung at the first pitch. "Strike one!" called the umpire. The next pitch was a ball. Kate swung hard at the third pitch, and the ball soared away. She was afraid to look, so she just started to run as fast as she could. Suddenly, a loud cheer went up from her team's bench.

9. When Kate stepped up to the plate, she was probably unhappy because

Ⓐ her team was losing.
Ⓑ it was the end of the game.
Ⓒ they had no runners on base.
Ⓓ Kate was not a good player.

10. Kate was probably scared because

Ⓐ she was not a good player.
Ⓑ her team was ahead.
Ⓒ she needed to hit the ball.
Ⓓ her ankle hurt.

11. When the game was over, Kate probably

Ⓐ went to first base.
Ⓑ ran to home plate.
Ⓒ felt very happy.
Ⓓ felt very sad.

12. A good title for this story could be

Ⓐ Ninth Inning Problem.
Ⓑ Running Home.
Ⓒ An Unhappy Team.
Ⓓ Kate Saves the Day.

13. Write what you think happened next in the story. Use complete sentences.

____

____

____

____

Name ______________________ Date ____________

Consonant Sounds

Directions Say each picture name. Write the letter that stands for the first sound.

Directions Say each picture name. Write the letter that stands for the last sound.

9. ______	10. ______	11. ______	12. ______
13. ______	14. ______	15. ______	16. ______

Name ______________________________ Date ______________

Consonant Blends

Directions Read each sentence below. Darken the circle next to the word that completes the sentence.

1. Tall trees give us ___.

Ⓐ spade Ⓑ grade Ⓒ wade Ⓓ shade

2. The new house is made of ___.

Ⓐ stick Ⓑ thick Ⓒ trick Ⓓ brick

3. The good news made her ___.

Ⓐ smile Ⓑ style Ⓒ spill Ⓓ slide

4. A hero is very ___.

Ⓐ gave Ⓑ slave Ⓒ brave Ⓓ shave

5. It's so hot that I think I'll go for a ___.

Ⓐ trim Ⓑ swim Ⓒ grim Ⓓ dim

6. When you are tired, you should ___.

Ⓐ nest Ⓑ rest Ⓒ best Ⓓ test

7. Little children like to play in the ___.

Ⓐ sand Ⓑ land Ⓒ hand Ⓓ wand

8. When it is dark, it is not ___.

Ⓐ tight Ⓑ night Ⓒ fight Ⓓ light

9. You can close a gate by using a ___.

Ⓐ patch Ⓑ latch Ⓒ batch Ⓓ match

10. Paper is very easy to ___.

Ⓐ sold Ⓑ cold Ⓒ bold Ⓓ fold

Name ______________________ Date ____________

Long and Short Vowel Sounds

Directions Say each picture name. Write the letter that stands for the vowel sound.

1. ______	**2.**  ______	**3.**  ______	**4.**  ______
5. 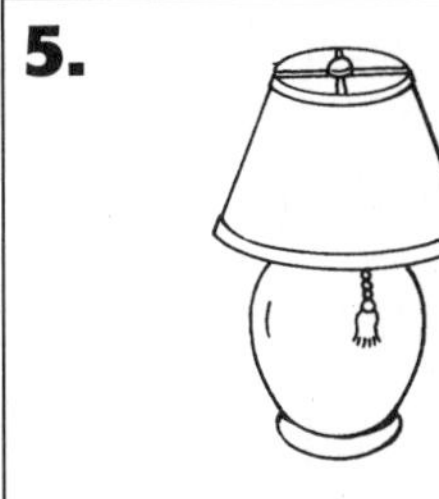 ______	**6.**  ______	**7.**  ______	**8.** 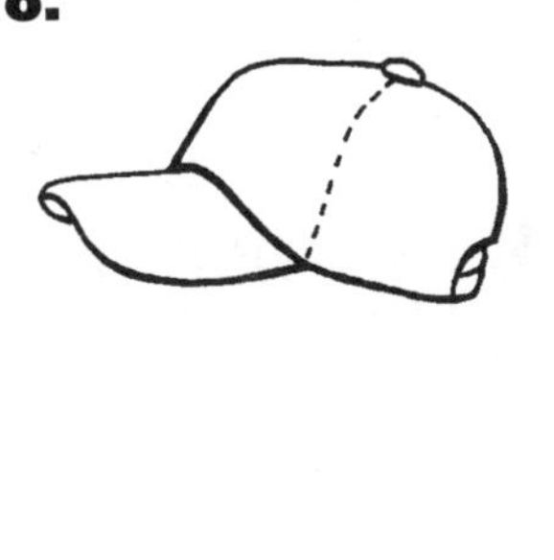 ______
9.  ______	**10.** 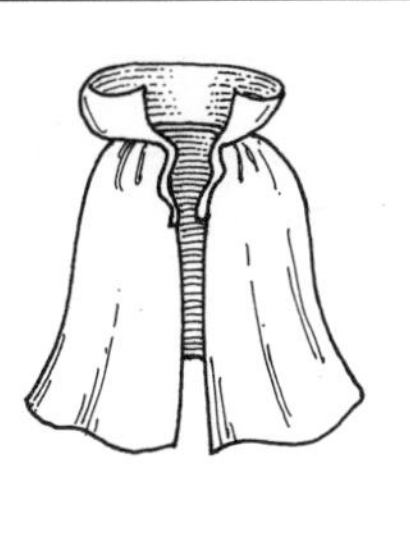 ______	**11.**  ______	**12.** 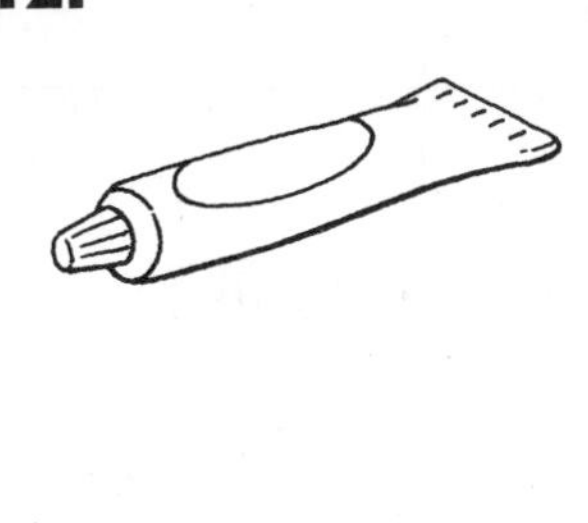 ______
13.  ______	**14.**  ______	**15.**  ______	**16.** 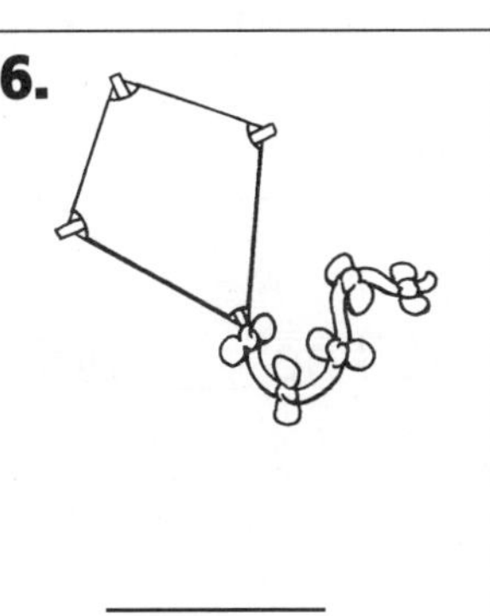 ______

Name ______________________________ Date ______________

More Vowel Sounds

Directions Read each sentence. Fill in the circle next to the word that completes the sentence.

1. Mort lives on a ___.	○ fern ○ farm ○ far
2. He plants seeds in the ___.	○ dirt ○ darn ○ dart
3. He loads up his ___.	○ cord ○ cart ○ curl
4. Mort has ___.	○ hurts ○ horns ○ horses
5. Mort has a ___ of cows.	○ hard ○ herd ○ hire
6. Mort ___ his hand.	○ hurt ○ here ○ horn
7. The ___ helps him.	○ north ○ nerve ○ nurse
8. At day's end, he rests on the ___.	○ porch ○ part ○ perk

Name ______________________ Date ____________

Word Meaning

Directions Read each meaning. Darken the circle for the word that fits the meaning.

1. having a high price

Ⓐ craze
Ⓑ expensive
Ⓒ automobile

2. very old

Ⓐ ancient
Ⓑ expensive
Ⓒ sequoia

3. to find out or learn

Ⓐ concentrate
Ⓑ discover
Ⓒ invent

4. a book

Ⓐ spine
Ⓑ volume
Ⓒ dune

5. the means of moving something from one place to another

Ⓐ transportation
Ⓑ spectators
Ⓒ turnpikes

6. a journey made for a definite purpose

Ⓐ circumference
Ⓑ expedition
Ⓒ transportation

7. keep from decaying

Ⓐ frame
Ⓑ preserve
Ⓒ succeed

8. send forcefully up or out

Ⓐ pace
Ⓑ sag
Ⓒ launch

9. a sea animal with a single shell

Ⓐ bivalve
Ⓑ univalve
Ⓒ cell

10. set free

Ⓐ release
Ⓑ tinker
Ⓒ preserve

Name ______________________ Date ____________

Word Meaning in Context

Directions Darken the circle for the word that fits in the blank.

1. I took ___ with my new camera.

Ⓐ books Ⓒ coins
Ⓑ records Ⓓ pictures

2. The speaker stood on the ___.

Ⓐ platform Ⓒ school
Ⓑ news Ⓓ plant

3. The clouds looked ___ and gloomy.

Ⓐ grade Ⓒ grape
Ⓑ grain Ⓓ gray

4. My mother has a good ___ for fudge cake.

Ⓐ friend Ⓒ recipe
Ⓑ dessert Ⓓ reason

5. The letter was sent to the wrong ___.

Ⓐ admire Ⓒ advance
Ⓑ address Ⓓ admit

6. We went out on the lake in a ___.

Ⓐ candle Ⓒ cannot
Ⓑ camp Ⓓ canoe

7. The books are too ___ to put in a backpack.

Ⓐ heat Ⓒ health
Ⓑ heavy Ⓓ hear

8. We made a ___ for dinner at the new restaurant.

Ⓐ mention Ⓒ reservation
Ⓑ catcher Ⓓ troop

9. Margie is a very ___ artist.

Ⓐ main Ⓒ talking
Ⓑ talented Ⓓ last

10. Nate showed us how to do the first ___.

Ⓐ excellent Ⓒ exact
Ⓑ example Ⓓ exit

Name ______________________ Date ______________

Words with Multiple Meanings

Directions Darken the circle for the word that fits both meanings.

1. something to sleep in
a place to grow flowers

Ⓐ bed Ⓒ soil
Ⓑ cot Ⓓ bag

2. a measurement
a place to play

Ⓐ inch Ⓒ yard
Ⓑ foot Ⓓ park

3. grows on a cornstalk
what we hear with

Ⓐ toe Ⓒ kernel
Ⓑ ear Ⓓ drum

4. dates grow on this kind of tree
a part of the hand

Ⓐ oak Ⓒ palm
Ⓑ finger Ⓓ nail

5. the season after winter
a coil made of metal

Ⓐ spring Ⓒ wire
Ⓑ summer Ⓓ fall

6. used to style hair
on top of a rooster's head

Ⓐ mousse Ⓒ comb
Ⓑ brush Ⓓ feather

7. used to mail a letter
put your foot down hard

Ⓐ walk Ⓒ dance
Ⓑ address Ⓓ stamp

8. a kind of snake
a baby's toy

Ⓐ cobra Ⓒ rattle
Ⓑ block Ⓓ garter

9. wear it on a finger
the sound of a bell

Ⓐ ring Ⓒ buzz
Ⓑ mitten Ⓓ chime

10. it cools the air
someone who roots for a team

Ⓐ wind Ⓒ fan
Ⓑ coach Ⓓ rain

Name ______________________ Date ______________

Antonyms

Directions Darken the circle for the word that means the opposite of the underlined word.

1. after

Ⓐ sooner
Ⓑ later
Ⓒ before
Ⓓ earlier

2. deep

Ⓐ well
Ⓑ wide
Ⓒ broad
Ⓓ shallow

3. polite

Ⓐ sloppy
Ⓑ happy
Ⓒ rude
Ⓓ firm

4. crooked

Ⓐ straight
Ⓑ sharp
Ⓒ across
Ⓓ path

5. lead

Ⓐ children
Ⓑ chase
Ⓒ run
Ⓓ follow

6. This magic trick always works.

Ⓐ often
Ⓑ never
Ⓒ soon
Ⓓ sometimes

7. That is wonderful news!

Ⓐ sad
Ⓑ great
Ⓒ terrible
Ⓓ old

8. The cupboard is bare.

Ⓐ clean
Ⓑ empty
Ⓒ dirty
Ⓓ full

9. Could you wrap that gift?

Ⓐ return
Ⓑ open
Ⓒ accept
Ⓓ send

10. This light is very dim.

Ⓐ bright
Ⓑ soft
Ⓒ shiny
Ⓓ weak

Name ______________________ Date ____________

Synonyms

Directions Darken the circle for the word that means the same or almost the same as the underlined word.

1. huge

Ⓐ large
Ⓑ tree
Ⓒ strong
Ⓓ building

2. above

Ⓐ road
Ⓑ walk
Ⓒ threw
Ⓓ over

3. tale

Ⓐ story
Ⓑ tablet
Ⓒ stove
Ⓓ teacher

4. student

Ⓐ book
Ⓑ write
Ⓒ pupil
Ⓓ pen

5. injure

Ⓐ just
Ⓑ journey
Ⓒ hurt
Ⓓ help

6. She told us a brief story.

Ⓐ short
Ⓑ sad
Ⓒ long
Ⓓ funny

7. What is your reply?

Ⓐ reason
Ⓑ word
Ⓒ answer
Ⓓ question

8. The boys exchanged baseball cards.

Ⓐ bought
Ⓑ traded
Ⓒ sold
Ⓓ wanted

9. She gave him an honest answer.

Ⓐ false
Ⓑ truthful
Ⓒ long
Ⓓ strange

10. She assisted her neighbor.

Ⓐ helped
Ⓑ saw
Ⓒ called
Ⓓ met

Name ______________________ Date ______________

Classifying

Directions

Darken the circle by the word that does not belong with the other words in the group.

1. Ⓐ hammer
Ⓑ saw
Ⓒ table
Ⓓ screwdriver

2. Ⓐ people
Ⓑ hand
Ⓒ arm
Ⓓ foot

3. Ⓐ April
Ⓑ Friday
Ⓒ Monday
Ⓓ Thursday

4. Ⓐ chocolate
Ⓑ ice cream
Ⓒ vanilla
Ⓓ strawberry

5. Ⓐ cow
Ⓑ horse
Ⓒ pig
Ⓓ fish

Directions

Darken the circle by the word that should be added to each group of words.

6. red, black, purple, ___

Ⓐ game
Ⓑ brown
Ⓒ book
Ⓓ doll

7. car, train, bus, ___

Ⓐ plane
Ⓑ farm
Ⓒ store
Ⓓ table

8. shoes, socks, shirt, ___

Ⓐ hair
Ⓑ paper
Ⓒ spoon
Ⓓ dress

9. one, fifty, four, ___

Ⓐ song
Ⓑ number
Ⓒ sixteen
Ⓓ face

10. oranges, peaches, plums, ___

Ⓐ houses
Ⓑ rooms
Ⓒ days
Ⓓ apples

Name ______________________________ Date ______________

Analogies

Directions Think about how the first two words are related. Write the word that completes the sentence.

1. Cow is to milk as hen is to ______________________.

   corn egg feather

2. Bark is to dog as quack is to ______________________.

   duck doctor moo

3. Bear is to cave as bee is to ______________________.

   honey buzz hive

4. Dog is to puppy as cat is to ______________________.

   kitten mouse yarn

5. Day is to night as hot is to ______________________.

   dark light cold

6. Mother is to father as aunt is to ______________________.

   son uncle cousin

7. Tall is to short as thick is to ______________________.

   thin shoe brick

8. House is to people as nest is to ______________________.

   door twigs birds

9. Deer is to antlers as goat is to ______________________.

   hoof horns tail

10. Fish is to scales as fox is to ______________________.

    fur socks pole

Name ______________________ Date ____________

Affixes and Compound Words

Directions

Darken the circle for the word that has a <u>prefix</u> or <u>suffix</u>.

1. Ⓐ happy
Ⓑ power
Ⓒ unfair
Ⓓ sentence

2. Ⓐ preheat
Ⓑ any
Ⓒ sample
Ⓓ color

3. Ⓐ lesson
Ⓑ napkin
Ⓒ science
Ⓓ cheerful

4. Ⓐ correct
Ⓑ helpless
Ⓒ many
Ⓓ daytime

5. Ⓐ camel
Ⓑ notebook
Ⓒ taller
Ⓓ picture

Directions

Darken the circle for the <u>compound</u> word.

6. Ⓐ outside
Ⓑ colorful
Ⓒ under
Ⓓ example

7. Ⓐ coldest
Ⓑ sometime
Ⓒ speaker
Ⓓ student

8. Ⓐ over
Ⓑ remember
Ⓒ spelling
Ⓓ baseball

9. Ⓐ running
Ⓑ tomorrow
Ⓒ mailbox
Ⓓ useful

10. Ⓐ possible
Ⓑ thunderstorm
Ⓒ kindness
Ⓓ counting

Name ______________________ Date ______________

Facts

Directions Read the story. Darken the circle for the answer that best completes the sentence.

Seashells come in many different shapes, sizes, and colors. Some shells grow as big as four feet long. The smallest shells are only half an inch long. Some shells have two sides that open like wings. Other shells are shaped like a curling tube. Shells come in many colors: white, black, brown, yellow, green, red, orange, and pink. They are like a rainbow in the ocean.

Many seashells are named for other things we know. The spider shell is one example. The spider shell has long points that look like spider legs. The comb shell has points, too. Its points are straight and close together, just like those in a comb.

There are two kinds of bear shells. One is called the little bear. It is a small shell. The bear-paw shell is different. It is a big shell with two parts. Each half looks like an animal foot.

1. Some shells grow

Ⓐ rainbows.
Ⓑ four feet long.
Ⓒ butterfly wings.

2. The smallest shells are only

Ⓐ half a foot long.
Ⓑ two inches wide.
Ⓒ half an inch long.

3. Some shells are named for

Ⓐ people who found them.
Ⓑ other things we know.
Ⓒ where they are found.

4. Some seashells have

Ⓐ arms.
Ⓑ points.
Ⓒ homes.

5. There are

Ⓐ two kinds of bear shells.
Ⓑ three types of butterflies.
Ⓒ two kinds of apple shells.

6. The bear-paw shell has

Ⓐ one part.
Ⓑ two parts.
Ⓒ three parts.

Name ______________________ Date ______________

Sequence

Directions Darken the circle by the sentence that should come first.

1. Ⓐ Each plant is set in its muddy bed by hand.
Ⓑ The farmer is barefoot as he walks in the wet fields.
Ⓒ In Asia rice is grown in large, wet fields.
Ⓓ The rice fields are called paddies.

2. Ⓐ The potatoes were ready to be harvested.
Ⓑ The machine stuck its iron fingers down under the potato plants.
Ⓒ The farmer used the new potato digger.
Ⓓ It lifted out a clump of dirt and potatoes.

3. Ⓐ Next spring their buds will open and grow into leaves.
Ⓑ The bare trees are now ready for winter.
Ⓒ Food is stored in their roots and branches.
Ⓓ The leaves will give us summer shade.

Directions Darken the circle by the sentence that should come last.

4. Ⓐ Then, he rested his head on the desk.
Ⓑ He covered his mouth with his hand as he yawned.
Ⓒ He leaned back on his chair and stretched his arms.
Ⓓ Manuel was very tired.

5. Ⓐ She represented hope.
Ⓑ It was the Statue of Liberty.
Ⓒ In 1886 the people of France gave the United States a very special gift.
Ⓓ Today, more than one hundred years later, Miss Liberty is still a symbol of freedom to the world.

6. Ⓐ He threw something silvery on the river bank.
Ⓑ The bear had caught a fish with his big, hairy paw.
Ⓒ The bear kept his eyes on the water.
Ⓓ Then, quick as a wink, his paw struck the water.

Name ______________________________ Date ______________

Context

Directions Darken the circle for the correct answer.

1. Juliette Gordon Low started the Girl Scouts in America. She had heard about the Boy Scouts. She thought it would be a good idea for girls, too. She believed that girls should learn more than just cooking. They should **explore** the outdoors and take care of themselves while doing so. In 1912 there were 18 Girl Scouts. Now there are 3 million Girl Scouts!

In this story the word **explore** means ___

Ⓐ walk. Ⓑ travel. Ⓒ paint.

---

2. On New Year's Day in China, there is a parade. People dress up and march down the street. A **special** part is the Lion Dance. The lion in the dance is not a real lion. Two people wear a lion suit. One person is the head. The other person is the body. Together they make the lion run, jump, paw the air, and wag its tail.

In this story the word **special** means ___

Ⓐ important. Ⓑ necessary. Ⓒ happy.

---

3. Cars burn gas in order to go. People burn food instead. You burn about two teaspoons of sugar when you walk a mile. But if you ride a bike, you can **extend** the distance. You can go five miles on two teaspoons of sugar! The wheels do the work instead of your feet.

In this story the word **extend** means ___

Ⓐ double. Ⓑ make longer. Ⓒ make shorter.

---

4. Cats and owls can see at night. But no animal can see in **complete** darkness. People and animals see because of light coming into their eyes. Some animals, like cats and owls, can see in very little light. The light can be so dim that people can't see at all.

In this story the word **complete** means ___

Ⓐ between. Ⓑ little. Ⓒ total.

Name ______________________ Date ____________

Main Idea

Directions Darken the circle by the best title for each paragraph.

1. We had been waiting on the sidewalk for a long time. Suddenly we heard a band playing. Many colorful floats came behind the band. All of the people on the floats waved to the crowd.

Ⓐ Watching a Parade
Ⓑ Waiting on the Sidewalk
Ⓒ Waving to the Crowd
Ⓓ Floating Down the Avenue

2. Dean had heard stories about elves, but he had never known that they were such tiny creatures. The elf he saw had an old, wrinkled face. He was dressed in a black coat, knee pants, and a broad-brimmed black hat. He was looking at a toy he was making on the workbench. He didn't know that Dean was watching him.

Ⓐ Stories About Elves
Ⓑ Dean Sees an Elf
Ⓒ Making Toys
Ⓓ The Young Elf

3. The loaves in pans move on a special belt to the steam box. As the pans go slowly through the steam box, the dough gets lighter. When the loaves are ready to be baked, they go to the oven. Bread is taken from the oven when it has baked.

Ⓐ The Steam Box
Ⓑ Making Dough Lighter
Ⓒ Many Loaves of Bread
Ⓓ How Bread Is Baked

4. Most beavers live in lodges that are built in pools in small streams and ponds. The lodges are made of sticks and mud. Some of them are several feet high. A part of the beaver lodge always stays above the water, but the entrance is always covered by water.

Ⓐ Beaver Lodges
Ⓑ How Beavers Cut Down Trees
Ⓒ Tall Beaver Lodges
Ⓓ Using Sticks and Mud

Name ______________________________ Date ______________

Conclusion

Directions Read the story. Darken the circle for the phrase that best completes the sentence.

1. Many sunken ships lie on the ocean floor. It is hard to raise them. One man found a way. He uses many small balls. Each ball is filled with air so that it floats. He runs a pipe through the inside of the ship. Then he forces the balls through the pipe. Soon the balls fill the ship, and the ship slowly rises.

From this story you can tell

Ⓐ the man was paid well for his idea.

Ⓑ the balls are colored blue like the sea.

Ⓒ the air in each ball helps raise the ship.

---

2. Most houses are made of wood, nails, and bricks. But a family in California wanted a house that was different. So they built their house with foam. They laid big sheets of plastic on the ground. Then they used fans to blow air under the sheets. When the sheets looked like large balloons, the family covered the sheets with foam. After the foam dried, they painted it the color of rocks.

From this story you can tell

Ⓐ the house looked like a rocky hill.

Ⓑ the house was painted blue and white.

Ⓒ part of the house was made of bricks.

---

3. The first year of life is very important for babies. During this time they eat their first food. They take their first steps. They say their first words. Babies also grow very fast. They gain about two pounds a month. They also grow ten inches taller. If a child grew this fast every year, a ten-year-old child would be ten feet tall!

From this story you can tell

Ⓐ older children grow slower than babies.

Ⓑ people stop learning things after age ten.

Ⓒ some ten-year-olds are very, very tall.

Name ______________________ Date ______________

Inference

Directions Read the story. Darken the circle for the sentence that best answers the question.

1. One orange is left in the bowl. You touch and smell it. The orange feels soft and mushy. It has a sharp smell. Part of the skin is broken. There is something white and powdery on the skin. You decide not to eat the orange.

Which of these sentences is probably true?

Ⓐ Eating the orange may make you sick.
Ⓑ The orange is not ripe yet.
Ⓒ The orange should be used for juice.

---

2. The Brooklyn Bridge links Brooklyn and Manhattan in New York. It is very long. The bridge hangs from long steel cables that are 16 inches thick. Two huge towers hold up the cables. The bridge has six lanes for cars and trucks.

Which of these statements is probably true?

Ⓐ The bridge can hold many cars and trucks.
Ⓑ The Brooklyn Bridge is the world's largest bridge.
Ⓒ The bridge is never used by people.

---

3. American settlers had a hard time moving west. They had to travel over mountains and through thick forests. For years they followed small trails made by Native Americans. In 1811 the government made one of the trails into a road. People could then go all the way from Maryland to Illinois. You can still travel from Washington, D.C., to St. Louis, Missouri, on this road.

Which of these sentences is probably true?

Ⓐ Some roads were once small trails.
Ⓑ Roads are hard to build.
Ⓒ Native Americans helped build the road.

Name ______________________________ Date ______________

A Bear Scare

Beaver talked his friend Skunk into going camping in the woods. Beaver had camped many times, but this would be Skunk's first camping trip. Beaver was an expert camper and told Skunk that he would set up their campsite.

Skunk tried to help, but he could not find anything that he could do right. Beaver cut down trees for shelter and for firewood. Then Skunk knocked over the stack of firewood. They went to catch fish for dinner, and Beaver caught a fish. Skunk only caught an old tin can. Skunk decided he was a terrible camper and wanted to stay for only one night.

During the night, Beaver and Skunk woke up when they heard a loud noise. A fierce growl came from the bushes near the shelter. Beaver was terribly frightened. Skunk told Beaver not to worry and crawled out of the shelter. Skunk carefully walked toward the noise.

"Who is there?" asked Skunk.

"Growl!" something answered.

Skunk quickly turned and sprayed the bushes with his horrible-smelling spray. Suddenly their friend Bear came out of the bushes coughing. Beaver and Skunk scolded Bear for scaring them. Beaver invited Skunk to go camping with him on every camping trip.

Skunk was pleased. "I might be a good camper after all," Skunk thought to himself as he fell asleep.

Go on to the next page.

Name ______________________ Date ______________

A Bear Scare, p. 2

Directions Answer each question about the story. Darken the circle for the correct answer.

1. Who goes on his first camping trip?

Ⓐ Beaver
Ⓑ Skunk
Ⓒ Bear
Ⓓ Skunk's friend

2. Why does Skunk dislike camping?

Ⓐ He cannot do anything right.
Ⓑ Beaver does everything.
Ⓒ It is scary.
Ⓓ Skunk becomes homesick.

3. Who makes the noise that wakes Skunk and Beaver?

Ⓐ Skunk
Ⓑ Beaver
Ⓒ the wind
Ⓓ Bear

4. What does Beaver think about Skunk?

Ⓐ Skunk is very brave.
Ⓑ Skunk is a bad camper.
Ⓒ Skunk is not brave.
Ⓓ Skunk knows how to fish.

5. What is something else that Skunk might be good at doing on a camping trip?

Ⓐ mountain climbing
Ⓑ collecting berries
Ⓒ sledding
Ⓓ building a cabin

Name ______________________ Date ____________

Trading Places

A little bird sat on the windowsill. He looked longingly into the house at a bird in its cage. The cage seemed to be such a pleasant place. It had a swing for exercise, a round reflecting mirror, and a little bell that made a sweet sound. There was always water in one dish and food and treats in another. The little bird thought it looked like a wonderful place to live.

Meanwhile, the bird in its cage looked at the world outside his window. He wondered what it would be like to fly free in the sky and land wherever he wanted. He wished he could see what lay beyond his neat backyard and the fence that surrounded it. His people were kind, but he couldn't help feeling the urge to fly out the window and be free.

One day, the people left both the window and the cage door open. The caged bird decided this was his chance. He quickly flew out the window and into the world beyond. At the same time, the free bird flew from the windowsill into the cage. At first, both birds were thrilled. But soon the house bird missed his cage. It was frightening outside! He wasn't sure where to look for food. Besides, the worms and bugs that the other birds were eating almost ruined his appetite! The outside bird felt trapped in the cage. His heart began to beat wildly. All he could think about was getting back outside!

At the first opportunity, both birds returned to their old ways. Now the caged bird looked at the world with new eyes. It was beautiful, but he was happy to look from his perch in the cage. As for the outside bird, he no longer wished to be in the cage. He could hardly believe that he had almost given up his precious freedom for that little space!

Go on to the next page.

Name ______________________ Date ______________

Trading Places, p. 2

Directions Answer the questions in complete sentences.

1. What was on the windowsill?

____

____

____

2. Why did the cage look like a wonderful place to live?

____

____

____

3. How did the caged bird get out of the cage?

____

____

____

4. Why didn't the house bird like the outside?

____

____

____

5. Why didn't the outside bird like the cage?

____

____

____

Name ______________________ Date ______________

Name Game

The Syms children had always wanted a dog. They asked their parents several times, and their parents told the children that a dog would need good care. The children promised their parents that they would take good care of a dog by themselves. Since there were five of them, the children were sure that this would not be a problem. Finally, the parents took the family to the animal shelter, and they chose a furry, white dog.

Now the children had to choose a name that everyone liked. Tim, the oldest, thought Neptune was a good name. Irene suggested the name Sport. Grace wanted to call the dog Button. Edward thought that Button was silly; he liked the name Scout. Rachel, the youngest, wanted to name the dog Spice.

Then Tim came up with an idea. "Let's use the first letter of each of our own names to name the dog," he said.

"I will agree if we start with the youngest and end with the oldest," said Rachel.

"R-E-G-I-T," said Irene. "That's not a name!"

"No, it isn't, but the letters T-I-G-E-R spell a name," said Grace.

The children agreed that Tiger would be a good name for the dog.

Go on to the next page.

Name ______________________________ Date ______________

Name Game, p. 2

Directions Answer each question about the story. Darken the circle for the correct answer.

1. What do the parents say about having a dog?

Ⓐ They cannot find one they like.
Ⓑ A dog needs good care.
Ⓒ They do not know where to find a dog.
Ⓓ They do not know where to keep the dog.

2. What problem do the children have, once they find a dog?

Ⓐ how to take the dog home
Ⓑ how to choose a name for the dog
Ⓒ deciding whom the dog belongs to
Ⓓ learning what kind of dog they have chosen

3. Tim comes up with the idea of ___.

Ⓐ pulling names out of a hat
Ⓑ letting the youngest family member name the dog
Ⓒ using letters from all of their names
Ⓓ not naming the dog

4. The children finally decide on the name ___.

Ⓐ Whitney
Ⓑ Sport
Ⓒ Regit
Ⓓ Tiger

5. Why is agreeing on a name important to the children?

Ⓐ The dog is everyone's pet.
Ⓑ They promised their parents they would take care of the dog.
Ⓒ They have never named a dog before.
Ⓓ They didn't like the name the dog had before they got it.

Name ______________________________ Date ______________

The Candlemaker

There once was a candlemaker from Brighton who made wonderful candles of all colors, shapes, and sizes. People came from near and far to admire and buy his candles. The candlemaker enjoyed making his candles so much that it did not seem right to ask people to pay for them. He gave candles away until there was none left to give.

One day, he reached into his cupboard for more dye, and there was none. He searched for more tallow, and there was none. He found string for the wick. However, without tallow or dye he could not make any candles. He had given away his last candle, and he did not know what to do.

He went to see his friend the woodcutter.

"I have no candles to give to people," he said, "You will need to work very hard to chop wood today. People will depend on the light from their fireplaces." It was soon known throughout the country that there were no more beautiful candles to be bought in Brighton.

That evening, neighbors arrived with the woodcutter. They brought tallow and dye for the candlemaker. He was surprised and pleased. The candlemaker asked them why they had brought supplies.

"You have been giving us candles for years," answered the woodcutter. "Brighton would no longer be bright if you stopped making candles."

Go on to the next page.

Name ______________________ Date ______________

The Candlemaker, p. 2

Directions Answer the questions in complete sentences.

1. Where was the candlemaker from?

2. Why did the candlemaker give his candles away?

3. What did the candlemaker use to make candles?

4. Why did people depend on light from candles and fireplaces in this story?

5. Will the candlemaker begin asking people to pay for candles? Why or why not?

Name ______________________ Date ______________

Elephants Rule!

Is the lion the "King of the Jungle?" The big cat certainly looks kingly. Other animals are afraid of it—and with good reason. Lions are great hunters. However, there is one animal that even lions fear. That animal is the elephant. The elephant fears nothing.

Long ago, there were about 350 kinds of elephants. They lived on every continent. Now only two kinds are left. They are the African elephant and the Asian, or Indian, elephant. The African elephant is the largest animal that lives on land. From trunk to tail, it is 25 feet long. It stands 13 feet high at the shoulders. It weighs more than eight tons. The Asian elephant is smaller. It is about 20 feet long and stands 10 feet high. It weighs "only" about five tons.

Big animals have big appetites. In the wild, an adult elephant eats 400 to 600 pounds of food every day. It drinks about 40 gallons of water. It sucks up the water with its trunk. Then it squirts the water into its mouth.

That big trunk is good for other reasons, too. An elephant has a very good sense of smell. Using its trunk and tusks, it can lift heavy loads. It can take the branches and bark off trees. It can even pull trees out of the ground, roots and all. Finally, it can use its trunk to make its trumpeting call.

TA-DAHHHH! Imagine hearing that sound in the jungle. No wonder other animals dash off! Even a lion will slink away into the bush.

Go on to the next page.

Name ______________________ Date ______________

Elephants Rule, p. 2

Directions Answer each question about the story. Darken the circle for the correct answer.

1. What animal do lions fear?

Ⓐ crocodiles
Ⓑ elephants
Ⓒ tigers
Ⓓ mice

2. How many kinds of elephants are left?

Ⓐ 35
Ⓑ 20
Ⓒ 350
Ⓓ 2

3. What is the largest animal that lives on land?

Ⓐ the "King of the Jungle"
Ⓑ the Asian elephant
Ⓒ the African elephant
Ⓓ the whale

4. How tall is the African elephant?

Ⓐ 13 feet
Ⓑ 400 feet
Ⓒ 8 feet
Ⓓ 20 feet

5. What is something else that an elephant might do with its trunk?

Ⓐ store things
Ⓑ change a tire
Ⓒ pick up food to eat
Ⓓ see tiny objects

Name ______________________ Date ______________

Wild Weather!

Weather is made up of many things. Temperature, water, wind, air pressure, clouds, and sunshine are all a part of it. In some places, the weather barely changes from one month to the next. In other places, it can change from hour to hour!

Changes in weather are usually not a big problem. But sometimes, the different things that make up weather can combine to cause dangerous storms.

A hurricane begins as a tropical storm. It becomes a hurricane when its winds reach 75 miles per hour. As it moves, the storm gets stronger. By the time it is a killer storm, its center, or eye, is much smaller than when it started to spin. The air pressure inside the eye is very low. Outside the eye, winds howl at up to 150 miles per hour. Heavy rains can fall up to two inches per hour. Hurricanes tend to stay out to sea. But they often cause much damage to areas along the coast. Buildings are turned into rubble. Boats are thrown into the air. A hurricane can last from four to 14 days. Eventually, it moves inland or over colder water. Then it will slow and die.

A tornado begins with the same kind of weather that causes a thunderstorm. Warm air meets cold air. The atmosphere becomes unstable. Some of the clouds begin to spin. A funnel forms and reaches downward. The wind speed in a tornado can reach 370 miles per hour. Most tornadoes last less than an hour. They travel about 20 miles. Over the ocean, they may form a waterspout. Over the desert, they cause a column of sand called a sand devil. On land, the worst tornadoes can take a house off its foundation. They can lift animals high into the sky and toss cars into the next block!

Go on to the next page.

Name ______________________ Date ______________

Wild Weather!, p. 2

Directions Answer the questions in complete sentences.

1. What are three things that make up weather?

____

____

____

2. When does a tropical storm become a hurricane?

____

____

____

3. Why does a hurricane cause so much damage?

____

____

____

4. How does a tornado form?

____

____

____

____

5. What are different names for tornadoes?

____

____

____

Name ______________________ Date ______________

Language Arts Overall Assessment

Directions Read each sentence. Darken the circle for the part of the sentence that has an error. Darken the circle for *E. none* if the sentence is correct.

	A	B	C	D	E
1.	Wendy and	her family	moved to	Miami, florida.	none
2.	"Yes,	I want	to go,	said Carlos.	none
3.	Mrs. Garcia	droved	Juan's friend	to school.	none
4.	Jody, do	you want to	go swimming	with us?	none
5.	I would like	to have a kitten,	a puppy, or	an hamster.	none
6.	He is	the most fastest	runner	in our class.	none
7.	Them	had been	trying to	go shopping.	none
8.	She said,	"that's a	very dangerous	trick!"	none
9.	Thanksgiving is	on the fourth	Thursday	in november.	none
10.	We visit	the Grand Canyon	in Arizona	last summer.	none

Go on to the next page.

Name ______________________ Date ______________

Language Arts Overall Assessment, p. 2

Directions Match the reference source or book part with its description.

1. dictionary

2. encyclopedia

3. atlas

4. thesaurus

5. table of contents

6. title page

a. Use this to find maps.

b. Use this to find synonyms and antonyms of words.

c. Use this to find the name of the book and the author.

d. Use this to find the meanings and pronunciations of words.

e. Use this to find facts on many subjects.

f. Use this to find the chapters or units in a book.

Directions Match the type of writing with its description.

7. personal narrative

8. information paragraph

9. how-to paragraph

10. descriptive paragraph

11. persuasive paragraph

12. friendly letter

g. has a heading, greeting, body, closing, and signature

h. tells the writer's feelings and asks the reader to agree

i. tells about the writer and uses the words *I*, *me*, and *my*

j. uses word pictures to tell what someone or something is like

k. uses details to tell facts about the main idea, or topic

l. tells how to do or make something

Directions Put these four words in ABC order.

13. tall test stone stand

__________ __________ __________ __________

Name ______________________ Date ____________

Capitalization

Directions Darken the circle for the part of the sentence that needs a capital letter. Darken the circle for *E. none* if the sentence <u>does not</u> need a capital letter.

	A	B	C	D	E
1.	did	you watch	television	last night?	none
2.	Don's sister,	susan,	is a very	good singer.	none
3.	My family	went to	hawaii	last summer.	none
4.	The book	report is	due next	Thursday.	none
5.	We go	back to	school	in september.	none
6.	We saw	mr. Green	at the store	today.	none
7.	Jim's	favorite book	is	Black beauty.	none
8.	Why don't	you and i	make dinner	tonight?	none
9.	Sara said,	"my mother	bakes the	best cookies."	none
10.	I read	a very good	book by	Judy blume.	none

Name ______________________ Date ____________

Capitalization

Directions Darken the circle for the part of the passage that needs a capital letter. Darken the circle for *D. none* if the passage does not need a capital letter.

1. Ⓐ My sister Ellie is learning
Ⓑ to ice-skate. she practices
Ⓒ for two hours each week.
Ⓓ none

2. Ⓐ Gina goes to
Ⓑ dancing school
Ⓒ every wednesday afternoon.
Ⓓ none

3. Ⓐ Rosita and i will
Ⓑ help Ms. Seng
Ⓒ unpack the new library books.
Ⓓ none

4. Ⓐ St. John, New brunswick,
Ⓑ is where you can see
Ⓒ the Reversing Falls.
Ⓓ none

5. Ⓐ Who is your favorite
Ⓑ author? Mine is
Ⓒ Dr. Seuss.
Ⓓ none

6. Ⓐ Rose has a new pet.
Ⓑ It is a canary. She
Ⓒ named it tweetie.
Ⓓ none

7. Ⓐ My mother asked, "who
Ⓑ wants to go downtown
Ⓒ with me this afternoon?"
Ⓓ none

8. Ⓐ My friend Dorrie costello
Ⓑ will be nine years old
Ⓒ on her next birthday.
Ⓓ none

9. Ⓐ It was so hot
Ⓑ last july that we
Ⓒ couldn't wait for summer
to end.
Ⓓ none

10. Ⓐ We celebrate thanksgiving
Ⓑ every November. It is
Ⓒ my favorite holiday.
Ⓓ none

Name ______________________________ Date ______________

Punctuation

Directions Darken the circle for the punctuation mark that makes the sentence correct. Darken the circle for *E. none* if no punctuation mark is needed.

1. Don't touch that sharp knife

Ⓐ ? Ⓒ . Ⓔ none
Ⓑ ; Ⓓ !

2. Doreen, please hand me the scissors

Ⓐ ! Ⓒ . Ⓔ none
Ⓑ : Ⓓ ,

3. You need eggs flour, and sugar to make a cake.

Ⓐ , Ⓒ " Ⓔ none
Ⓑ " Ⓓ !

4. Thank you for the gift

Ⓐ ? Ⓒ , Ⓔ none
Ⓑ . Ⓓ "

5. "What do you think of that" she asked.

Ⓐ ? Ⓒ , Ⓔ none
Ⓑ . Ⓓ "

6. When will you visit Paris, France

Ⓐ , Ⓒ ! Ⓔ none
Ⓑ . Ⓓ ?

7. It's too good to be true!

Ⓐ ? Ⓒ ' Ⓔ none
Ⓑ ; Ⓓ ,

8. "Have a happy birthday! he exclaimed.

Ⓐ . Ⓒ " Ⓔ none
Ⓑ ? Ⓓ ,

9. James ordered cereal, eggs, and toast.

Ⓐ ? Ⓒ " Ⓔ none
Ⓑ , Ⓓ .

10. What time is it?" asked Jeff.

Ⓐ ? Ⓒ ! Ⓔ none
Ⓑ , Ⓓ "

Name ________________________ Date ______________

Punctuation

Directions Darken the circle for the line that has a punctuation error. Darken the circle for *D. none* if the sentence does not have any errors.

1. Ⓐ Terri got a really
Ⓑ cute poddle for her birthday.
Ⓒ She named him Frisky?
Ⓓ none

2. Ⓐ Mr. Chan asked, "Who
Ⓑ wants to try to do this
Ⓒ science experiment?"
Ⓓ none

3. Ⓐ Mrs. Smiths garden
Ⓑ is the prettiest one
Ⓒ on our street.
Ⓓ none

4. Ⓐ My mother always uses
Ⓑ apples, bananas peaches,
Ⓒ and oranges in fruit salad.
Ⓓ none

5. Ⓐ Have you ever
Ⓑ visited Niagara Falls
Ⓒ near Buffalo New York?
Ⓓ none

6. Ⓐ Ian said, "Let's
Ⓑ play a game of
Ⓒ basketball after school.
Ⓓ none

7. Ⓐ My aunt is coming
Ⓑ to visit. I want to
Ⓒ show her my school.
Ⓓ none

8. Ⓐ Dear Tina
Ⓑ Thank you for the
Ⓒ set of watercolors.
Ⓓ none

9. Ⓐ When is your sister
Ⓑ going to start taking
Ⓒ voice lessons.
Ⓓ none

10. Ⓐ Mr. Locata, our math
Ⓑ teacher taught us how to
Ⓒ to check our subtraction.
Ⓓ none

Name ______________________ Date ______________

Capitalization and Punctuation

Directions Darken the circle for the sentence that has correct capitalization and punctuation.

1. Ⓐ Let's go to the Bronx Zoo.
Ⓑ let's go to the bronx Zoo.
Ⓒ Let's go to the bronx Zoo.
Ⓓ let's go to the Bronx zoo.

2. Ⓐ mr. J. T. White left Sunday.
Ⓑ Mr. J. T. White left Sunday.
Ⓒ Mr. j. t. White left sunday.
Ⓓ Mr. J T White left Sunday.

3. Ⓐ is the library open today?
Ⓑ is the Library open today?
Ⓒ Is the Library open today.
Ⓓ Is the library open today?

4. Ⓐ No I can't play soccer.
Ⓑ No, I can't play soccer.
Ⓒ "No I can't play, soccer.
Ⓓ No" I can't play soccer.

5. Ⓐ Carla lives on elm Street.
Ⓑ carla lives on Elm Street.
Ⓒ Carla lives on Elm Street.
Ⓓ carla lives on elm Street.

6. Ⓐ it's a beautiful day.
Ⓑ it's a beautiful day!
Ⓒ It's a beautiful day.
Ⓓ it's a beautiful day?

7. Ⓐ I like to paint, said Rosa
Ⓑ "I like to paint," said Rosa.
Ⓒ I like to paint," said Rosa.
Ⓓ I like to paint said Rosa.

8. Ⓐ Jim's brother will visit in march.
Ⓑ Jim's brother will visit in March.
Ⓒ Jims brother will visit in March.
Ⓓ jim's brother will visit in March.

9. Ⓐ did you visit europe.
Ⓑ Did You visit Europe!
Ⓒ did you visit europe?
Ⓓ Did you visit Europe?

10. Ⓐ Isn't that Dr. Fine?
Ⓑ Isnt that Dr Fine.
Ⓒ Isn't that dr fine!
Ⓓ isnt that Dr. Fine?

Name ______________________ Date ______________

Verbs

Directions Darken the circle for the word or words that best fit the sentence.

1. We like to ___ home from school.

Ⓐ walked Ⓒ walks
Ⓑ walking Ⓓ walk

2. Marci ___ in the school office.

Ⓐ working Ⓒ had working
Ⓑ did worked Ⓓ works

3. My best friend ___ coming home with me.

Ⓐ is Ⓒ will
Ⓑ are Ⓓ can't

4. Justin ___ the drums in the band.

Ⓐ did played Ⓒ have played
Ⓑ playing Ⓓ played

5. The gray squirrel ___ up and down the tree.

Ⓐ runned Ⓒ ran
Ⓑ run Ⓓ running

6. Mr. Scott ___ the school band next year.

Ⓐ will leading Ⓒ has leaded
Ⓑ will lead Ⓓ did lead

7. Shawn ___ his fish every day.

Ⓐ has feeded Ⓒ did fed
Ⓑ fed Ⓓ have feed

8. The children ___ turns going down the slide.

Ⓐ took Ⓒ have took
Ⓑ taken Ⓓ taked

9. Chelsea ___ the scraps of paper in the basket.

Ⓐ throwed Ⓒ had throwing
Ⓑ has threw Ⓓ threw

10. On their way to the park, they ___ Max.

Ⓐ seen Ⓒ had saw
Ⓑ have saw Ⓓ saw

Name ______________________ Date ______________

Pronouns

Directions Darken the circle for the word that can be used in place of the underlined word or words.

1. Did Rhea finish her homework?

Ⓐ it Ⓒ they
Ⓑ she Ⓓ he

2. Tanya invited Lola and me to her piano recital.

Ⓐ our Ⓒ we're
Ⓑ they Ⓓ us

3. Jemma wrote a letter to Maida.

Ⓐ she Ⓒ they
Ⓑ her Ⓓ he

4. You and I have to go shopping later.

Ⓐ Us Ⓒ We
Ⓑ Our Ⓓ She

5. Robin and Kyle are members of the swim team.

Ⓐ They Ⓒ Them
Ⓑ Our Ⓓ Their

6. This morning Kevin hit a home run.

Ⓐ them Ⓒ we
Ⓑ him Ⓓ he

7. Please give Sandy and me the homework assignment.

Ⓐ I Ⓒ we
Ⓑ us Ⓓ they

8. Debbi and Jamie are setting the table.

Ⓐ They Ⓒ We
Ⓑ Them Ⓓ Their

9. Ms. Velez will visit us this afternoon.

Ⓐ They Ⓒ She
Ⓑ Her Ⓓ He

10. The puppy is very furry.

Ⓐ It Ⓒ They
Ⓑ We Ⓓ Us

Name ______________________ Date ____________

Using Words Correctly

Directions

Darken the circle for the word or words that best complete each sentence.

1. Ricky feels ___ today than he felt yesterday.

Ⓐ bestest Ⓒ bested
Ⓑ better Ⓓ best

2. Stan is the ___ boy in our class.

Ⓐ taller Ⓒ shorted
Ⓑ tallest Ⓓ shorter

3. The water dripped ___ into the bowl.

Ⓐ slow Ⓒ slowly
Ⓑ slowing Ⓓ slower

4. Harry is the ___ boy I know.

Ⓐ happiest Ⓒ most happiest
Ⓑ happy Ⓓ happier

5. My sister is ___ than I am.

Ⓐ oldest Ⓒ older
Ⓑ more old Ⓓ old

Directions

Darken the circle for the line that has an error in the way the words are used. Darken the circle for *D. No mistakes* if there is no error.

6. Ⓐ My sister Tiffany she always
Ⓑ likes to play
Ⓒ with her dolls.
Ⓓ No mistakes

7. Ⓐ Because there was a traffic jam,
Ⓑ our bus was more than
Ⓒ a hour late getting us to school.
Ⓓ No mistakes

8. Ⓐ Sal didn't want
Ⓑ nobody to know where
Ⓒ he was going after school.
Ⓓ No mistakes

9. Ⓐ Throw them broken cups
Ⓑ into the trash bin before
Ⓒ someone gets hurt.
Ⓓ No mistakes

10. Ⓐ Larry wanted to eat at
Ⓑ MacDiner, but his mother
Ⓒ wouldn't give him no money.
Ⓓ No mistakes

Name ______________________ Date ______________

Sentence Parts

Directions Darken the circle for the simple subject.

1. The cup had a broken handle.
   Ⓐ The Ⓑ cup Ⓒ broken Ⓓ handle

2. Ruth handed me the blue paper.
   Ⓐ Ruth Ⓑ handed Ⓒ blue Ⓓ paper

3. She came in first in the race.
   Ⓐ She Ⓑ came Ⓒ first Ⓓ race

4. This summer the boys will go to camp.
   Ⓐ summer Ⓑ boys Ⓒ go Ⓓ camp

5. When will the bus leave the station?
   Ⓐ will Ⓑ bus Ⓒ leave Ⓓ station

Directions Darken the circle for the simple predicate.

6. The music class began at five o'clock.
   Ⓐ music Ⓑ began Ⓒ five Ⓓ o'clock

7. Their new telephone cost more than the old one.
   Ⓐ new Ⓑ telephone Ⓒ cost Ⓓ old

8. Her new shoes shine very brightly.
   Ⓐ shoes Ⓑ shine Ⓒ very Ⓓ brightly

9. Charlie quickly answered the question.
   Ⓐ Charlie Ⓑ quickly Ⓒ answered Ⓓ question

10. The giant plane landed on the runway.
    Ⓐ giant Ⓑ plane Ⓒ landed Ⓓ runway

Name ______________________ Date ______________

Clear Sentences

Directions Darken the circle for the sentence that is written most clearly.

1. Ⓐ A thick bushy tail.
Ⓑ The squirrel has a thick bushy tail.
Ⓒ A thick bushy tail has the squirrel.
Ⓓ The squirrel a thick bushy tail has.

2. Ⓐ When the wind it blew, the apples.
Ⓑ The wind it blew, the apples down.
Ⓒ When the wind blew, the apples fell.
Ⓓ The apples they fell when the wind blew.

3. Ⓐ It was time to go home for the children.
Ⓑ To go home for the children it was time.
Ⓒ For the children to go home it was time.
Ⓓ It was time for the children to go home.

4. Ⓐ In the bush a nest had a brown bird.
Ⓑ A brown bird had a nest in the bush.
Ⓒ A nest in a bush had a brown bird.
Ⓓ In the bush had a brown bird a nest.

5. Ⓐ When they heard a noise did they stop.
Ⓑ They stopped when they heard a noise.
Ⓒ A noise they heard so when they stopped.
Ⓓ They heard a noise stopped they did.

6. Ⓐ In the spring the grass it is green.
Ⓑ The grass in the spring.
Ⓒ In the spring the grass is green.
Ⓓ Green is the grass in the spring.

Name ________________________ Date ____________

Spelling

Directions Read each sentence. If one of the words is misspelled, darken the circle for that word. If all the words are spelled correctly, then darken the circle for *D. No mistake*.

1. Callie played a <u>livly</u> <u>tune</u> on her <u>piano</u>. <u>No mistake</u>
   Ⓐ Ⓑ Ⓒ Ⓓ

2. Everyone <u>laughed</u> at the <u>funny</u> <u>story</u>. <u>No mistake</u>
   Ⓐ Ⓑ Ⓒ Ⓓ

3. Jake told the <u>scaryest</u> <u>ghost</u> story at <u>camp</u>. <u>No mistake</u>
   Ⓐ Ⓑ Ⓒ Ⓓ

4. <u>Potatoes</u> are a <u>starchy</u> <u>vegtible</u>. <u>No mistake</u>
   Ⓐ Ⓑ Ⓒ Ⓓ

5. The <u>magical</u> king <u>granted</u> the shoemaker three <u>wishs</u>. <u>No mistake</u>
   Ⓐ Ⓑ Ⓒ Ⓓ

6. We saw some <u>unusual</u> <u>butterflies</u> in the <u>woods</u>. <u>No mistake</u>
   Ⓐ Ⓑ Ⓒ Ⓓ

7. We are <u>planning</u> to <u>climb</u> that <u>mountin</u>. <u>No mistake</u>
   Ⓐ Ⓑ Ⓒ Ⓓ

8. Don't <u>lean</u> <u>against</u> that <u>shelf</u>. <u>No mistake</u>
   Ⓐ Ⓑ Ⓒ Ⓓ

9. The car <u>startd</u> to <u>slide</u> on the icy <u>highway</u>. <u>No mistake</u>
   Ⓐ Ⓑ Ⓒ Ⓓ

10. In <u>sewing</u> <u>class</u> I am making an <u>aperun</u> for my mom. <u>No mistake</u>
   Ⓐ Ⓑ Ⓒ Ⓓ

Name ______________________________ Date ______________

Spelling

Directions Darken the circle for the correctly spelled word that fits the sentence.

1. Is that ___ new jacket?

Ⓐ yore
Ⓑ you're
Ⓒ your
Ⓓ youre

2. What is the ___ between these two books?

Ⓐ difference
Ⓑ diffrence
Ⓒ diffrince
Ⓓ diference

3. I have to return ___ books.

Ⓐ libary
Ⓑ liberry
Ⓒ library
Ⓓ librery

4. We live on planet ___.

Ⓐ Erth
Ⓑ Eirth
Ⓒ Eurth
Ⓓ Earth

5. ___ turn is it to serve snacks?

Ⓐ Who's
Ⓑ Whoos
Ⓒ Whose
Ⓓ Whoose

6. Our new ___ comes from Alaska.

Ⓐ neighbor
Ⓑ neighber
Ⓒ nayghbor
Ⓓ nieghbor

7. ___ new car is light blue.

Ⓐ They're
Ⓑ Their
Ⓒ There
Ⓓ Thier

8. Mrs. Ferris is our school crossing ___.

Ⓐ gaurd
Ⓑ guard
Ⓒ gard
Ⓓ guarde

9. Last ___ we went to the zoo.

Ⓐ Thersday
Ⓑ Thursday
Ⓒ Thuersday
Ⓓ Thuresday

10. Next ___ is a holiday.

Ⓐ Tusday
Ⓑ tuesday
Ⓒ Tuesday
Ⓓ Tuseday

Name ____________________ Date ____________

Spelling

Directions Learn to spell these words. Use each word in a sentence. Spell these words correctly in all your writing.

about	easy	little	raise	tomorrow
address	enough	loose	read	tonight
again	every	loving	receive	train
all right	fierce	making	remember	trouble
along	first	many	right	truly
already	forty	maybe	rough	until
always	fourth	mother	said	used
among	friend	name	says	vacation
because	getting	nice	school	very
been	goes	none	shoes	wear
before	guard	o'clock	since	weather
bought	guess	off	skis	weigh
busy	half	often	some	were
buy	haven't	once	soon	we're
choose	having	party	store	when
close	hear	peace	straight	where
come	heard	people	summer	which
coming	here	piece	sure	white
could	hour	played	teacher	whole
couldn't	house	plays	tear	would
country	instead	please	terrible	write
dear	knew	pretty	they	wrote
didn't	know	quarter	thought	your
does	laid	quit	through	you're
early	letter	quite	tired	

Name ______________________ Date ______________

Reference Materials

Directions Darken the circle for the correct answer.

1. You would probably use the ___ to find the meaning of a word.
   Ⓐ encyclopedia Ⓑ dictionary Ⓒ computer Ⓓ book

2. You would probably use the ___ to find a city in your state.
   Ⓐ index Ⓑ atlas Ⓒ dictionary Ⓓ thesaurus

3. The ___ in your health book would give the meaning of the word *illness*.
   Ⓐ glossary Ⓑ table of contents Ⓒ index Ⓓ title page

4. You would probably use the ___ to find a synonym for the word *sick*.
   Ⓐ index Ⓑ atlas Ⓒ encyclopedia Ⓓ thesaurus

5. To see if your health book has information on the common cold, you would look at the ___.
   Ⓐ glossary Ⓑ table of contents Ⓒ index Ⓓ title page

6. The word ___ would fall on a dictionary page with the guide words *hand/hiccup*.
   Ⓐ heart Ⓑ hospital Ⓒ habit Ⓓ high

7. A ___ graph compares data using bars of different heights or lengths.
   Ⓐ circle Ⓑ picture Ⓒ bar Ⓓ population

8. A ___ is a picture that shows the order of historical events.
   Ⓐ table Ⓑ time line Ⓒ web Ⓓ scan

9. To find information about a new kind of surgery, you would probably look in the ___ section of a computer directory.
   Ⓐ Games Ⓑ Health and Fitness
   Ⓒ Shopping Ⓓ Arts and Entertainment

Name ______________________ Date ______________

Parts of a Book

Directions Answer the questions.

ART PROJECTS AT THE BEACH by Sandy Shore Crafts Books, Inc.	**Contents** Getting Started 8 Shell Art 10 Sand Art 32 Sea-Plant and Rock Crafts 50	Beaches, 8–10, 26, 29 Plants, 50–54, 60–62 Rocks, 50–54, 59–62 Sands, 8–12, 32–49 Shells, 8, 10–30
title page	**table of contents**	**index**

1. What is the title of the book? ______________________

2. Who wrote the book? ______________________

3. What company published this book? ______________________

4. What is the first chapter in the book? ______________________

5. On what pages would you find facts about beaches?

____

6. On what page is Sand Art? ______________________

7. On what pages would you find facts about shells? ______________________

8. How many pages have information about plants? ______________________

9. Which part of the book would tell you where to find information about getting started? ______________________

10. Which two parts of the book tell you where to find information about rocks? ______________________

Name ______________________ Date ______________

ABC Order and Dictionary Skills

Directions Write these words in alphabetical order.

panda	bat	aardvark	deer	monkey
snake	tiger	frog	zebra	horse

1. ______________ 6. ______________

2. ______________ 7. ______________

3. ______________ 8. ______________

4. ______________ 9. ______________

5. ______________ 10. ______________

Directions Use the sample dictionary page to answer the questions.

stamp/track

stamp[1] [stamp] **n.** a mark or seal.

stamp[2] [stamp] **v.** to bring your foot down with force.

track[1] [trak] **n. 1.** marks left by a person, an animal, or a thing. **2.** a beaten trail. **3.** a pair of metal rails, as a train track.

track[2] [trak] **v.** to follow by using traces left behind. The dog will track the fox.

11. What are the guide words on this page? ______________

12. Which word means "a beaten trail"? ______________

13. Which words show more than one meaning? ______________

14. What is meaning 1 of **track**[1]? ______________

15. What part of speech is **stamp**[2]? ______________

Name ______________________ Date ____________

Charts and Graphs

Directions Darken the circle for the correct answer.

Kinds of Animals

Animal Group	Examples	Most Do This
Amphibians	Newts and frogs	Live in water and on land; lay eggs
Insects	Butterflies and bees	Have their skeletons on the outside; lay eggs
Mammals	Cows and mice	Have fur; young grow inside mother
Reptiles	Snakes and turtles	Are cold-blooded; lay eggs

1. Which animal group has fur?

Ⓐ amphibians
Ⓑ insects
Ⓒ mammals
Ⓓ reptiles

2. To which animal group do frogs belong?

Ⓐ amphibians
Ⓑ insects
Ⓒ mammals
Ⓓ reptiles

3. Which animals are reptiles?

Ⓐ newts and frogs
Ⓑ butterflies and bees
Ⓒ cows and mice
Ⓓ snakes and turtles

4. Which group does not lay eggs?

Ⓐ amphibians
Ⓑ insects
Ⓒ mammals
Ⓓ reptiles

Pie Sales

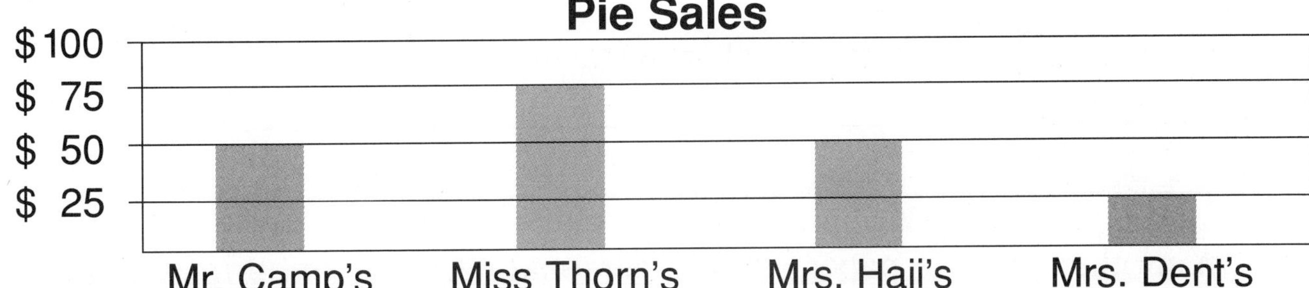

5. Whose class earned the most money?

Ⓐ Mr. Camp's
Ⓑ Miss Thorn's
Ⓒ Mrs. Haji's
Ⓓ Mrs. Dent's

6. Which two classes made $50?

Ⓐ Mr. Camp's and Mrs. Haji's
Ⓑ Miss Thorn's and Mrs. Haji's
Ⓒ Mr. Camp's and Mrs. Dent's
Ⓓ Mrs. Haji's and Mrs. Dent's

Name ______________________ Date ____________

Personal Narrative and Information Paragraph

Directions Label these sentences *beginning, middle,* or *ending.*

______________ **1.** A patch of lettuce grew under my window.

______________ **2.** I planted seeds under my window.

______________ **3.** Mom picked the lettuce for a salad.

Directions Read the information paragraph. Answer the questions that follow.

Animal tracks can tell you many things. For example, most cat tracks are smaller than dog tracks. Also, cat tracks are more rounded than dog tracks are. Cats usually keep their nails pulled in, but dogs can't do that. So dog tracks show nail marks.

4. What sentence tells the main idea of this paragraph? ______________

____

5. What are two details in the paragraph?

____

____

6. On another sheet of paper, write a personal narrative or an information paragraph.

Name ______________________ Date __________

Friendly Letter

Directions Read the letter. Answer the questions that follow.

324 Sunshine Drive
San Antonio, TX 78211
October 8, 2001

Dear Aunt Margaret,

I received the shirt you sent today. It is so pretty. Blue is my favorite color. I am going to wear it to school tomorrow. Thank you very much.

I can't wait to see you in December.

Much love,
Rosa

1. What is the purpose for writing this letter?

____

____

2. When was the letter written? How do you know?

____

____

3. Who wrote the letter? How do you know?

____

____

4. On another sheet of paper, write your own friendly letter.

Name ______________________ Date ____________

How-To Paragraph

Directions Read the how-to paragraph. Answer the questions that follow.

To tie-dye a shirt, start by bunching a white shirt in a ball and wrapping rubber bands tightly around it. Or, you might want to fold it back and forth like a fan and then wrap rubber bands around it. Next, soak the shirt in clear water. Then, place it in the dye. Let it soak for a few minutes. Remove it from the dye and rinse it until the water runs clear. Remove some of the rubber bands and put it in another color of dye. Finally, remove all the rubber bands to see your brightly colored, tie-dyed shirt.

1. What does this how-to paragraph teach?

____

____

____

2. List at least two words or phrases that tell time order.

____

____

3. What is the last step?

____

____

____

4. On another sheet of paper, write your own how-to paragraph.

Name ________________________________ Date ______________

Descriptive Paragraph

Directions Read the descriptive paragraph. Answer the questions that follow in complete sentences.

Lori picked up Casey's right leg and put it into the green pants. Casey squirmed and his leg came out of the pants.

"Do you not like those green pants?" Lori asked. She picked up the red and white striped pants. Casey lay still while Lori put the pants on him.

Then Lori picked up the blue hat with a red ball on top. She tied the hat under Casey's chin. Casey shook his head. Lori pulled Casey's tail out of the hole she'd cut in the pants.

"You look cute, Casey!" Lori said.

Casey said, "Meow."

1. What color pants would Casey not wear?

____

____

2. How did Lori make the pants fit Casey?

____

____

3. What two details tell you Casey is a cat?

____

____

____

4. On another sheet of paper, write your own descriptive paragraph.

Name ______________________ Date ____________

Persuasive Paragrah

Directions Read the persuasive paragraph. Answer the questions that follow.

The best building material for a house is bricks. A brick house always stays cool in summer and warm in winter. Houses made of wood need to be painted. Bricks never need to be painted. People get wet during the rainy season in a house made of straw. A brick house will keep people dry. Most importantly, a wolf cannot blow down a house made of bricks.

1. Draw a line under the topic sentence.

2. List the three main reasons the writer gives.

____

____

____

____

3. Which reason does the writer think is most important?

____

____

4. On another sheet of paper, write your own persuasive paragraph.

Name ______________________ Date ______________

Math Overall Assessment

Directions Darken the circle for the correct answer to each problem.

1. Which number tells how many base ten blocks are shown here?

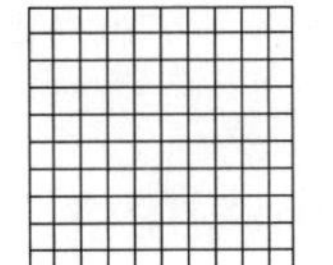 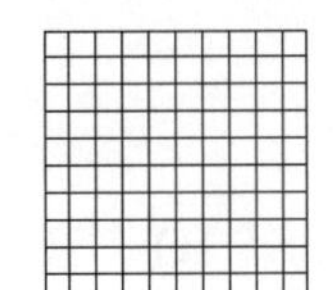 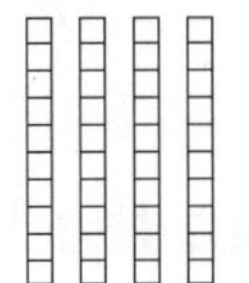

Ⓐ 24　　Ⓒ 240
Ⓑ 204　　Ⓓ 42

2. Which number is written in the box? Sixteen thousand, four

Ⓐ 16,004　　Ⓒ 6,400
Ⓑ 1,640　　Ⓓ 16,040

3. Which symbol belongs in the blank space?

Ⓐ star　　Ⓒ triangle
Ⓑ square　　Ⓓ circle

4.

$$\begin{array}{r} 107 \\ -\ 26 \\ \hline \end{array}$$

Ⓐ 101　　Ⓒ 81
Ⓑ 17　　Ⓓ 121

5.

$$\begin{array}{r} 35 \\ \times\ 3 \\ \hline \end{array}$$

Ⓐ 150　　Ⓒ 105
Ⓑ 305　　Ⓓ 915

6. $6 \div 3 =$

Ⓐ 3　　Ⓒ 9
Ⓑ 2　　Ⓓ none

7. $711 + 2 + 64 =$

Ⓐ 777　　Ⓒ 727
Ⓑ 707　　Ⓓ none

8. Which symbol belongs in the blank space?

$7 \_\_\_ 9 = 25 - 9$

Ⓐ +　　Ⓒ ×
Ⓑ –　　Ⓓ ÷

9. Which number tells how many angles there are in the kite?

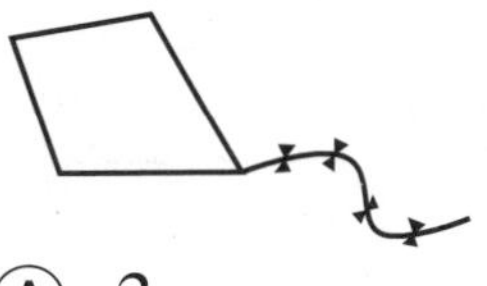

Ⓐ 3　　Ⓒ 7
Ⓑ 6　　Ⓓ 4

10. Which number is 213 rounded to the nearest ten?

Ⓐ 220　　Ⓒ 215
Ⓑ 210　　Ⓓ 200

Name ______________________ Date ______________

Math Overall Assessment, p. 2

Directions Write <, >, or =.

1. 3×4 ◯ 4×3 **2.** $\frac{1}{2}$ ◯ $\frac{3}{4}$ **3.** 1,203 ◯ 1,103

Directions Write the answers.

4. Put the weight of each shark in order from the least to the greatest. Write the weights on the lines.

______ ______ ______ ______ ______

5. $483 + 17 =$ ______

6. ______ $\times 8 = 48$

7. $3 \times 410 =$ ______

8. ● ▲ ■ ● ▲ ■ ● ______

9. \$5 – \$3.75 = ______

10. $56 \div$ ______ $= 7$

11. Name an activity you would do if it were 30° C.

____

12. Draw the hands on the clock to show 3:15.

Name ______________________ Date ____________

Number Concepts

Directions Darken the circle for the correct answer to each question.

1. Which number tells how many blocks are shown here?

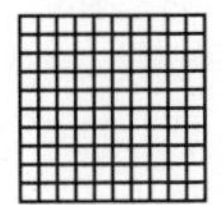 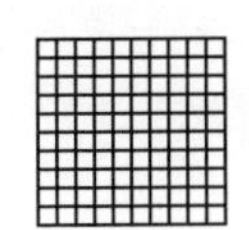 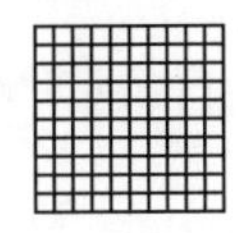 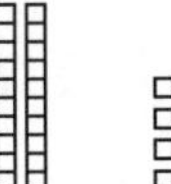 

Ⓐ 427　　Ⓒ 37
Ⓑ 327　　Ⓓ 307

2. Which of these numbers has a 6 in the tens place?

Ⓐ 6,623
Ⓑ 4,306
Ⓒ 3,650
Ⓓ 5,064

3. Which number is the same as three thousand four hundred thirty-five?

Ⓐ 3,435
Ⓑ 3,534
Ⓒ 4,335
Ⓓ 3,453

4. Which is another name for 8 hundreds, 0 tens, and 3 ones?

Ⓐ 830
Ⓑ 803
Ⓒ 83
Ⓓ 8,003

5. Which is another way to write 917?

Ⓐ 900 + 10 + 7
Ⓑ 900 + 7
Ⓒ 90 + 100 + 7
Ⓓ 90 + 10 + 7

6. Which is another way to write 6×3?

Ⓐ $6 \times 6 \times 6$
Ⓑ $3 + 3 + 3 + 3 + 3 + 3$
Ⓒ $18 \div 6$
Ⓓ $3 \times 3 \times 3$

7. Which number is an even number?

Ⓐ 25
Ⓑ 11
Ⓒ 7
Ⓓ 16

8. Which number is closest in value to 600 when rounded?

Ⓐ 60
Ⓑ 699
Ⓒ 602
Ⓓ 589

Name ______________________ Date ______________

Number Concepts

Directions Write the letter to tell which property is shown.

_____ **1.** $5 + 2 = 2 + 5$	**A.** Identity Property
_____ **2.** $0 \times 9 = 0$	**B.** Zero Property
_____ **3.** $7 \div 1 = 7$	**C.** Distributive Property
_____ **4.** $2 \times (4 + 3) = (2 \times 4) + (2 \times 3)$	**D.** Associative Property
_____ **5.** $3 + (7 + 8) = (3 + 7) + 8$	**E.** Commutative Property

Directions Write <, >, or =.

6. $6 + 14$ ◯ 6×14 **7.** $12 - 2$ ◯ $12 + 2$ **8.** 5×10 ◯ 4×10

9. $25 + 5$ ◯ 6×5 **10.** 7×1 ◯ $5 \div 5$ **11.** $17 - 8$ ◯ $8 + 1$

Directions Write the answers.

12. $5 \times 3 =$ ______________

13. $5 \times 30 =$ ______________

14. $5 \times 300 =$ ______________

Directions Write three other facts for this fact family. $7 + 3 = 10$

15. ______________________________

16. ______________________________

17. ______________________________

Name ______________________ Date ______________

Addition and Subtraction of Whole Numbers

Directions Darken the circle for the correct answer. Darken the circle for *D. None of these* if the correct answer is not given.

1. $7 + 3 + 5 =$

Ⓐ 15 Ⓒ 12
Ⓑ 14 Ⓓ None of these

2. $463 + 27 =$

Ⓐ 480 Ⓒ 490
Ⓑ 580 Ⓓ None of these

3.
$$\begin{array}{r} 483 \\ +\,217 \\ \hline \end{array}$$

Ⓐ 700 Ⓒ 600
Ⓑ 690 Ⓓ None of these

4. $\square + 62 = 65$

Ⓐ 4 Ⓒ 2
Ⓑ 3 Ⓓ None of these

5.
$$\begin{array}{r} 828 \\ +\,861 \\ \hline \end{array}$$

Ⓐ 1,689 Ⓒ 1,690
Ⓑ 1,609 Ⓓ None of these

6. $90 - 70 =$

Ⓐ 30 Ⓒ 20
Ⓑ 10 Ⓓ None of these

7. $73 - 14 =$

Ⓐ 67 Ⓒ 69
Ⓑ 59 Ⓓ None of these

8.
$$\begin{array}{r} 107 \\ -\,26 \\ \hline \end{array}$$

Ⓐ 101 Ⓒ 81
Ⓑ 17 Ⓓ None of these

9.
$$\begin{array}{r} 603 \\ -\,468 \\ \hline \end{array}$$

Ⓐ 35 Ⓒ 235
Ⓑ 291 Ⓓ None of these

10.
$$\begin{array}{r} 413 \\ -\,95 \\ \hline \end{array}$$

Ⓐ 418 Ⓒ 318
Ⓑ 328 Ⓓ None of these

Name ______________________ Date ______________

Multiplication and Division of Whole Numbers

Directions Darken the circle for the correct answer. Darken the circle for *D. None of these* if the correct answer is not given.

1. $\begin{array}{r} 7 \\ \times 6 \\ \hline \end{array}$

Ⓐ 12 Ⓒ 28
Ⓑ 30 Ⓓ None of these

2. $3 \times 312 =$

Ⓐ 636 Ⓒ 946
Ⓑ 936 Ⓓ None of these

3. $\begin{array}{r} 52 \\ \times 2 \\ \hline \end{array}$

Ⓐ 104 Ⓒ 94
Ⓑ 74 Ⓓ None of these

4. $8 \times 177 =$

Ⓐ 1,416 Ⓒ 916
Ⓑ 1,156 Ⓓ None of these

5. $5 \times 407 =$

Ⓐ 2,350 Ⓒ 2,035
Ⓑ 2,305 Ⓓ None of these

6. $8 \div 2 =$

Ⓐ 3 Ⓒ 6
Ⓑ 4 Ⓓ None of these

7. $3\overline{)27}$

Ⓐ 9 Ⓒ 8
Ⓑ 7 Ⓓ None of these

8. $64 \div 8 =$

Ⓐ 9 Ⓒ 6
Ⓑ 7 Ⓓ None of these

9. $4\overline{)35}$

Ⓐ 8 R3 Ⓒ 5 R3
Ⓑ 8 Ⓓ None of these

10. $3\overline{)60}$

Ⓐ 30 Ⓒ 20
Ⓑ 15 Ⓓ None of these

Name ______________________ Date ____________

Mixed Operations with Whole Numbers

Directions Darken the circle for the correct answer. Darken the circle for *D. None of these* if the correct answer is not given.

1. $423 + 18 =$

Ⓐ 431 Ⓒ 541
Ⓑ 421 Ⓓ None of these

2. $\begin{array}{r} 35 \\ \times 3 \\ \hline \end{array}$

Ⓐ 915 Ⓒ 105
Ⓑ 324 Ⓓ None of these

3. $\begin{array}{r} 200 \\ -45 \\ \hline \end{array}$

Ⓐ 135 Ⓒ 165
Ⓑ 155 Ⓓ None of these

4. $\square \times 8 = 48$

Ⓐ 8 Ⓒ 6
Ⓑ 7 Ⓓ None of these

5. $8 \div 7 =$

Ⓐ 1 R1 Ⓒ 1 R7
Ⓑ 1 Ⓓ None of these

6. $3 \times 410 =$

Ⓐ 1,250 Ⓒ 1,230
Ⓑ 1,240 Ⓓ None of these

7. $\begin{array}{r} 470 \\ -80 \\ \hline \end{array}$

Ⓐ 390 Ⓒ 410
Ⓑ 480 Ⓓ None of these

8. $7\overline{)210}$

Ⓐ 3 Ⓒ 5
Ⓑ 30 Ⓓ None of these

9. $2 \times 322 =$

Ⓐ 644 Ⓒ 544
Ⓑ 744 Ⓓ None of these

10. $5 \times 8 =$

Ⓐ 40 Ⓒ 45
Ⓑ 35 Ⓓ None of these

Name ______________________ Date ____________

Geometry

Directions Darken the circle for the correct answer to each question.

1. Which is an example of a closed curve?

Ⓐ S

Ⓑ L

Ⓒ D

Ⓓ G

2. Which two shapes are similar figures?

Ⓐ □ □

Ⓑ ○ ⬯

Ⓒ △ △

Ⓓ ⬡ ⬡

3. Look at the numbered shapes. Which two figures are congruent?

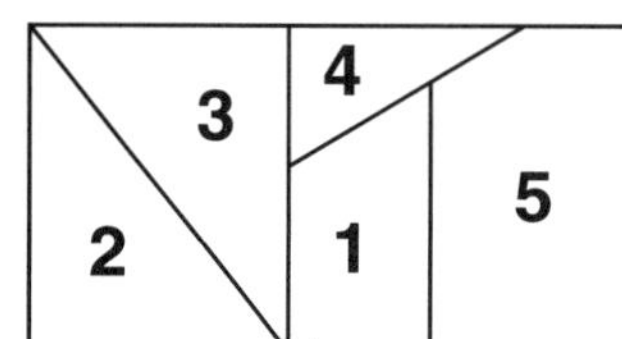

Ⓐ 1 and 5 Ⓒ 3 and 4

Ⓑ 2 and 3 Ⓓ 2 and 5

4. Which shape will not have a line of symmetry if it is folded on the dotted line?

Ⓐ

Ⓑ

Ⓒ

Ⓓ

Directions Write the number of faces, edges, and vertices.

5. ________ faces

________ edges

________ vertices

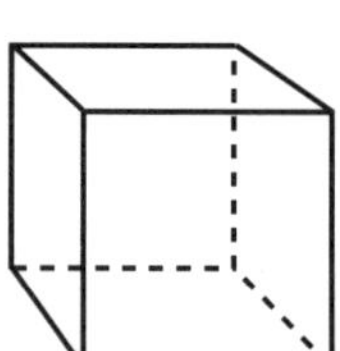

6. ________ faces

________ edges

________ vertices

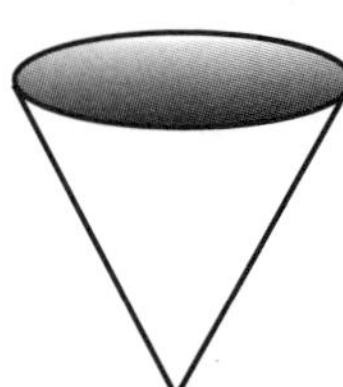

Name ______________________ Date ____________

Measurement

Directions Darken the circle for the correct answer to each problem. For 1–3 choose an appropriate measure.

1. distance of a field trip

Ⓐ mile Ⓒ yard
Ⓑ foot Ⓓ inch

2. amount of milk on cereal

Ⓐ L Ⓒ gal
Ⓑ mL Ⓓ tbsp

3. an elephant

Ⓐ oz Ⓒ g
Ⓑ mg Ⓓ kg

4. Which unit would you use to show length?

Ⓐ ounce Ⓒ pound
Ⓑ inch Ⓓ degree

5. Which unit is best to use to measure the weight of a crayon?

Ⓐ gram Ⓒ foot
Ⓑ pound Ⓓ liter

6. Carla bought a muffin for 49¢ and a glass of milk for 42¢. About how much money did Carla spend?

Ⓐ 80¢ Ⓒ 70¢
Ⓑ 60¢ Ⓓ 90¢

7. Katrina made a pitcher of juice. About how much juice was in the pitcher?

Ⓐ 20 quarts Ⓒ 2 cups
Ⓑ 2 quarts Ⓓ 200 cups

8. Andre measured the window so he could buy curtains. What is the best estimate of the height of the window?

Ⓐ 4 inches Ⓒ 40 feet
Ⓑ 4 feet Ⓓ 400 inches

9. Which temperature means the weather is very cold?

Ⓐ 65° F Ⓒ 38° F
Ⓑ 10° F Ⓓ 79° F

10. Which is a reasonable estimate for the height of a 10-year-old child?

Ⓐ 4 yd Ⓒ 4 ft
Ⓑ 7 yd Ⓓ 21 in.

Name ______________________ Date ____________

Fractions and Decimals

Directions Darken the circle by the correct answer to each problem.

1. Which figure is $\frac{2}{3}$ shaded?

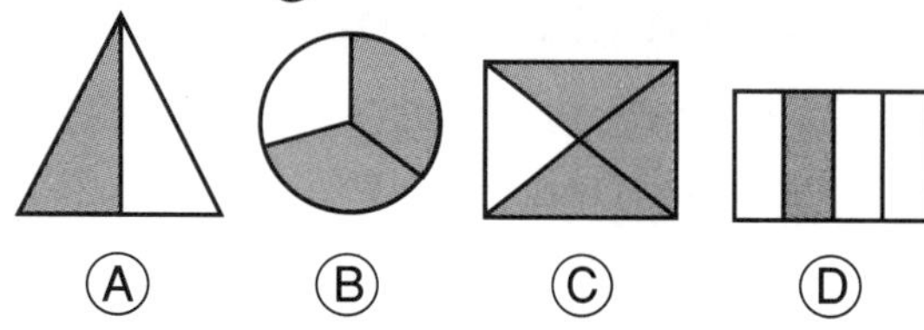

Ⓐ Ⓑ Ⓒ Ⓓ

2. Which fraction shows how much one part of this sandwich equals?

Ⓐ $\frac{1}{2}$ Ⓒ $\frac{1}{4}$

Ⓑ $\frac{1}{3}$ Ⓓ $\frac{2}{3}$

3. Which sign shows the relationship?

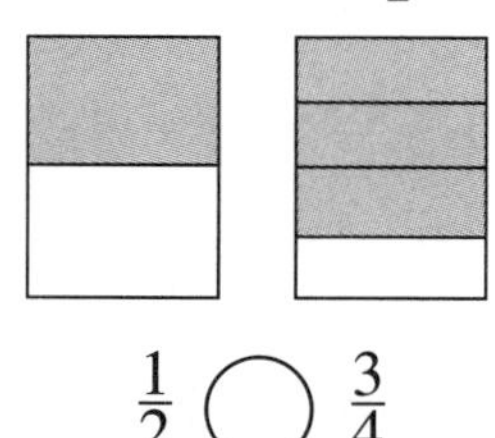

$\frac{1}{2}$ ◯ $\frac{3}{4}$

Ⓐ > Ⓒ =

Ⓑ < Ⓓ don't know

4. Which sign shows the relationship?

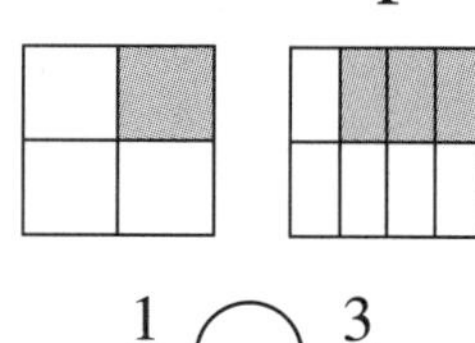

$\frac{1}{4}$ ◯ $\frac{3}{8}$

Ⓐ > Ⓒ =

Ⓑ < Ⓓ don't know

5. Which is the decimal for the shaded part of this picture?

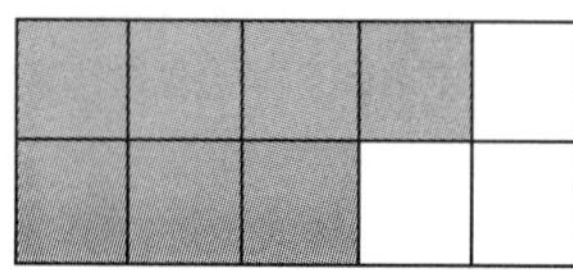

Ⓐ 0.4 Ⓒ 0.3

Ⓑ 3.0 Ⓓ 0.7

6. Which figure is 0.75 shaded?

Ⓐ 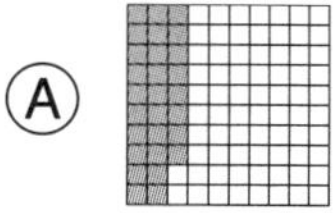 Ⓑ 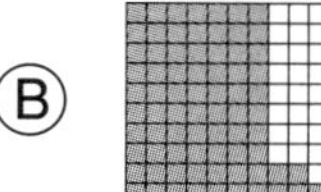

Ⓒ 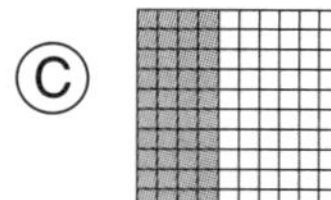 Ⓓ 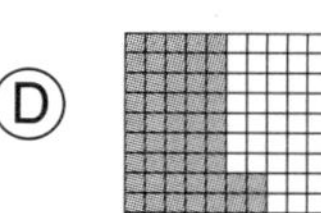

7. Which is the decimal numeral for one and six tenths?

Ⓐ 1.06 Ⓒ 10.6

Ⓑ 0.16 Ⓓ 1.6

8. $2.05 + $0.35 =

Ⓐ $2.40 Ⓒ $5.10

Ⓑ $5.55 Ⓓ $2.50

Name ______________________ Date ____________

Statistics and Probability

Directions Write the answers to the questions. Use the table.

Favorite Sports in Mr. Martinez's Class

Sport	Tally
Bowling	𝍸 |
Tennis	||||
Swimming	𝍸 |||
Basketball	𝍸 𝍸 𝍸
Football	𝍸 ||||

1. Which sport is most popular?

____

2. How many people like basketball and football?

____

3. How many people participated in this survey?

____

4. Take a survey of your class. Which sport is most popular?

____

Directions Darken the circle for the correct answer. Use the spinner.

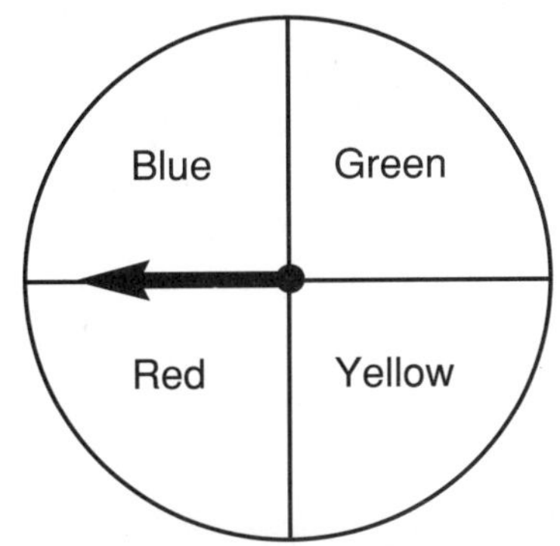

5. How many colors are there in the spinner?

Ⓐ 2 Ⓑ 4 Ⓒ 3

6. How many spaces are red?

Ⓐ 1 Ⓑ 2 Ⓒ 3

7. What are the chances that the arrow will stop on red?

Ⓐ 1 out of 3
Ⓑ 2 out of 4
Ⓒ 1 out of 4

8. What are the chances that the arrow will stop on blue?

Ⓐ 4 out of 1
Ⓑ 1 out of 4
Ⓒ 1 out of 2

Name ______________________ Date ____________

Pre-Algebra: Patterns

Directions Darken the circle for the missing number in each series.

1. 23, 25, 27, 29, ___

Ⓐ 28
Ⓑ 31
Ⓒ 32
Ⓓ 30

2. 70, 65, 60, 55, ___

Ⓐ 75
Ⓑ 59
Ⓒ 45
Ⓓ 50

3. 1, 3, ___, 7, 9

Ⓐ 6
Ⓑ 4
Ⓒ 5
Ⓓ 2

4. 36, ___, 54, 63, 72

Ⓐ 45
Ⓑ 40
Ⓒ 44
Ⓓ 46

5. 14, 21, 28, ___, 42

Ⓐ 30
Ⓑ 32
Ⓒ 35
Ⓓ 40

6. 699, 799, 899, 999, ___

Ⓐ 1,099
Ⓑ 1,999
Ⓒ 9,999
Ⓓ 9,990

7. 4, 2, 5, 2, 6, ___

Ⓐ 7
Ⓑ 3
Ⓒ 9
Ⓓ 2

8. ___, 9, 13, 17, 21

Ⓐ 3
Ⓑ 7
Ⓒ 5
Ⓓ 1

9. 1, 0, ___, 1, 0, 0

Ⓐ 0
Ⓑ 1
Ⓒ 2
Ⓓ 3

10. 100, 125, 150, ___, 200

Ⓐ 155
Ⓑ 165
Ⓒ 170
Ⓓ 175

Name ______________________________ Date ________________

Pre-Algebra: Patterns

Directions In each box is a pattern. Continue the pattern to show what comes next.

1.

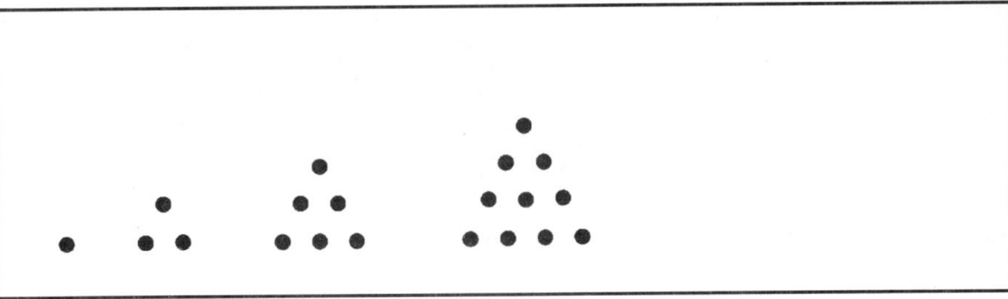

2.

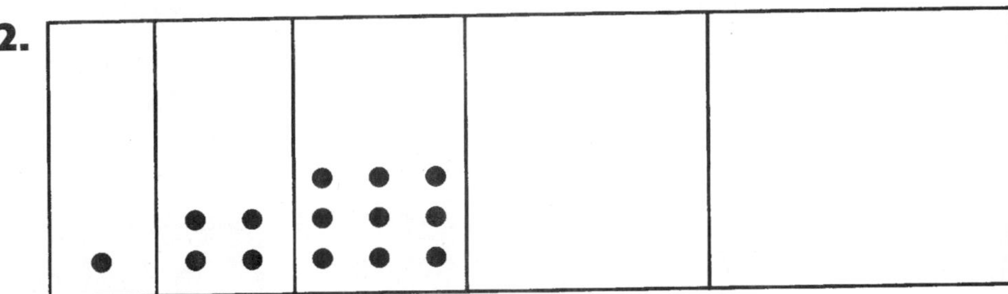

3.

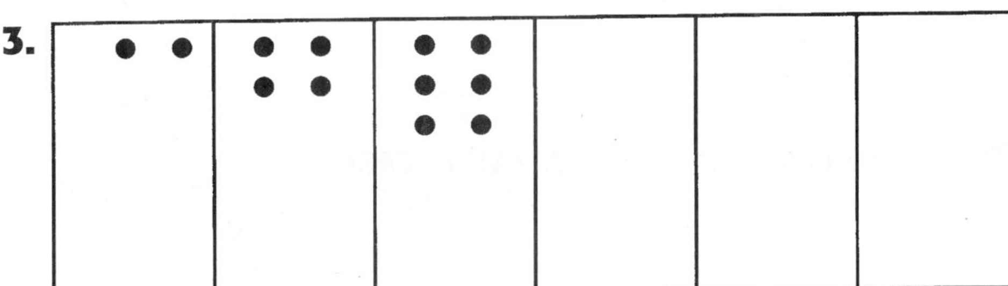

4.

3	5	7	9	____

5.

Name ______________________ Date ______________

Money

Directions Count the money and write the amount.

1.   ________

2.  ________

Directions Circle the letter beside the matching amount.

3. 	a. 	b. 	c. 
4. 	a. 	b. 	c. 

Directions List the coins and bills you would receive in change.

	Paid	Cost of Item	Change
5.		$0.42	________
6.		$2.47	________

Directions List the least number and type of coins you would receive from a $1 bill.

7.  $0.48

____

8.  $0.59

____

Name ______________________ Date ______________

Time

Directions Write the time that is shown on each clock.

1. 

____

2. 

____

3. 

____

Directions Write the time that it will be, or that it was, for each example.

4. 

7 minutes later

____

5. 

3 hours and
10 minutes later

____

6. 

2 hours and
10 minutes earlier

____

Directions Darken the circle by the correct answer.

7. Look at the clock. What will be the time in 25 minutes?

Ⓐ 7:10
Ⓑ 7:45
Ⓒ 8:15
Ⓓ 7:25

8. Which clock shows 6:45?

Ⓐ  

Ⓒ 

Ⓑ 

Ⓓ  

Name ______________________________ Date ______________

Estimation

Directions For 1–8, darken the circle for the correct answer.
For 9–10, write your estimate on the line.

1. Which is the best estimate of the temperature of a cup of hot chocolate?

Ⓐ 110° F Ⓒ 60° F
Ⓑ 22° F Ⓓ 75° F

2. Which of the following would you use to estimate 63 plus 22?

Ⓐ 70 and 20 Ⓒ 60 and 20
Ⓑ 70 and 30 Ⓓ 60 and 30

3. Which would take the longest time?

Ⓐ feeding a cat
Ⓑ walking to school
Ⓒ mailing a letter
Ⓓ drawing a circle

4. Which is the best estimate of the length of a piece of paper?

Ⓐ 11 inches Ⓒ 11 yards
Ⓑ 11 feet Ⓓ 11 miles

5. Which unit would you use to measure the water in an aquarium?

Ⓐ cup
Ⓑ pint
Ⓒ quart
Ⓓ gallon

6. Which unit would you use to measure the length of your desk?

Ⓐ centimeter
Ⓑ liter
Ⓒ kilometer
Ⓓ gram

7. Where do you live if it's 33° C in March?

Ⓐ Maine
Ⓑ Texas
Ⓒ Ohio
Ⓓ Colorado

8. Which animal has a weight closest to yours?

Ⓐ an elephant
Ⓑ a goldfish
Ⓒ a baby chicken
Ⓓ a medium-size dog

9. Estimate the length in inches.

10. Estimate the length in centimeters. ______________

Name ____________________ Date ____________

Problem Solving: Whole Numbers

Directions Darken the circle for the correct answer to each question.

1. Noriko made 46 cupcakes. Of the 46, 18 were chocolate. The other cupcakes were vanilla. How many vanilla cupcakes did she make?

Ⓐ 28 Ⓒ 63
Ⓑ 38 Ⓓ 66

2. The mailbox numbers on one wall of a building numbered from 849 to 916. Which mailbox number could be on that wall?

Ⓐ 925 Ⓒ 848
Ⓑ 879 Ⓓ 831

3. Terri has a new box of felt-tip markers. She has 3 red markers, 4 blue markers, and 3 green markers. How many markers does she have altogether?

Ⓐ 12 Ⓒ 10
Ⓑ 9 Ⓓ 11

4. Find the number below that is an even number. The digits total 15 when added together. Which number is it?

Ⓐ 492 Ⓒ 735
Ⓑ 583 Ⓓ 644

5. Helga bounces a ball 58 times. Sally bounces a ball 39 times. Which number sentence shows how to find how many more times Helga bounces the ball than Sally?

Ⓐ $\square - 58 = 39$
Ⓑ $58 - 39 = \square$
Ⓒ $58 + 39 = \square$
Ⓓ $\square \times 39 = 58$

6. Ava sells tickets at the movie theater. Each ticket costs $3. How much will she charge for 6 tickets?

Ⓐ $9 Ⓒ $12
Ⓑ $3 Ⓓ $18

7. There are 3 tennis balls in a can. How many cans of tennis balls will Pat need to buy if he needs 27 tennis balls?

Ⓐ 7 Ⓒ 9
Ⓑ 8 Ⓓ 24

Name ______________________ Date ____________

Problem Solving: Whole Numbers

Directions Solve each problem. Write the answer.

1. What is the product of the numbers that are in the triangle but not in the square?

____

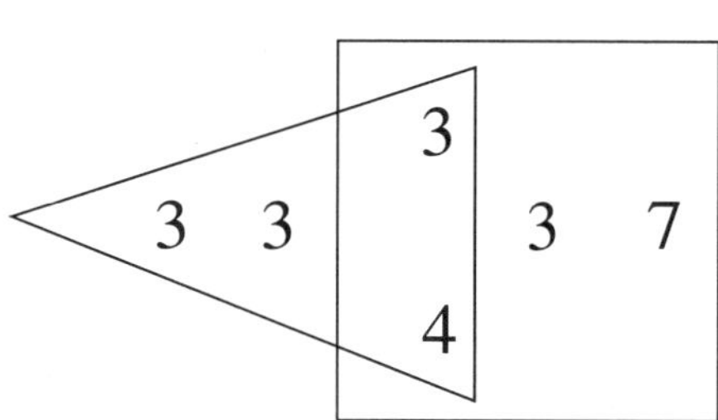

2. All week, the high temperature for each day has been 4° higher than the day before. On Monday, the temperature was 15° F. If the temperature continues to rise 4° each day, what will the temperature be on Sunday?

____

3. Toby and Travis are brothers. Toby is 3 years older than Travis. The sum of their ages is 37. How old is Toby?

____

4. Ella is taller than Mark but shorter than Dan. Dan is shorter than Ethan. Who is the tallest?

____

5. Sheo's bag of apples weighs 8 pounds more than his bag of oranges. The two bags weigh 24 pounds total. How much does the bag of apples weigh?

____

6. Find a 3-digit number that is greater than 400. The digits total 11 when they are added together. Which number is it?

____

7. Jack bought 2 piñatas for a party. He gave the sales clerk $35.00 and received $3.00 change. How much did each piñata cost?

____

8. Myra saw packages of coloring books for sale. Each package has 3 coloring books. How many coloring books are in 7 packages?

____

Name ______________________ Date ____________

Problem Solving: Measurement and Geometry

Directions

Darken the circle for the correct answer.

1. Carlo's back yard is 10 feet long and 28 feet wide. What is the perimeter of Carlo's yard?

Ⓐ 76 feet
Ⓑ 448 feet
Ⓒ 29 feet
Ⓓ 280 feet

2. What is the area of Carlo's back yard?

Ⓐ 256 square feet
Ⓑ 448 square feet
Ⓒ 86 square feet
Ⓓ 280 square feet

3. Derek has 15 erasers that are each 1 inch wide. His pencil box is 1 foot long. How many erasers can Derek place side by side in his pencil box?

Ⓐ 12 erasers
Ⓑ all of them
Ⓒ 9 erasers
Ⓓ none of them

Directions

Write the answer.

4. Kung paid for a box of crayons using 3 quarters, 1 dime, and 4 pennies. How much did he pay for the crayons?

____

5. The temperaure at Lana's house is 83° F. At the shore, it is 12° cooler. What is the temperature at the shore?

____

6. Yoko combines 875 mL of white paint and 250 mL of red paint. Does Yoko make more than or less than 1,000 mL of pink paint?

____

Name ______________________________ Date ______________

Problem Solving: Fractions and Decimals

Directions Darken the circle for the correct answer to each question.

1. A window has 5 equal parts. Bill must wash 3 of the parts, or three fifths. What fraction does he <u>not</u> wash?

Ⓐ $\frac{1}{5}$ Ⓒ $\frac{3}{5}$

Ⓑ $\frac{2}{5}$ Ⓓ $\frac{4}{5}$

2. Chuck gave $\frac{1}{4}$ of his sandwich to Inez, and he gave $\frac{2}{}$ of his sandwich to Frank. How much of his sandwich did Chuck give away?

Ⓐ $\frac{1}{4}$ Ⓒ $\frac{3}{4}$

Ⓑ $\frac{2}{4}$ Ⓓ all of it

3. Sheo has 18 markers. He gives $\frac{1}{6}$ of the markers to his sister. How many markers does he give his sister?

Ⓐ 3 Ⓒ 12

Ⓑ 6 Ⓓ 13

4. Hoa had 7 chocolate donuts and 5 plain donuts. She gave $\frac{1}{4}$ of the donuts to her friends. How many donuts did she have left?

Ⓐ 3 Ⓒ 7

Ⓑ 5 Ⓓ 9

5. Which set of coins is worth the most money?

Ⓐ 8 nickels

Ⓑ 2 quarters

Ⓒ 3 dimes

Ⓓ 45 pennies

6. Mariko needs 2 pairs of gloves. Each pair costs $6.00. Mariko has $9.78. How much more money does she need?

Ⓐ $3.78

Ⓑ $15.78

Ⓒ $3.22

Ⓓ $2.22

7. Kim swam 3 laps. Each lap was 10.3 meters long. How far did Kim swim?

Ⓐ 30.9 meters

Ⓑ 10.6 meters

Ⓒ 40.3 meters

Ⓓ 30.6 meters

8. Tia has a garden that is 4.2 meters by 3.2 meters. What is the perimeter of her garden?

Ⓐ 7.4 meters

Ⓑ 4.23 meters

Ⓒ 14.8 meters

Ⓓ 12.4 meters

Name ______________________________ Date ______________

Science Overall Assessment

Directions Darken the circle for the correct answer to complete each statement.

1. Nearly three fourths of Earth is covered by ___.

Ⓐ water Ⓒ air
Ⓑ land Ⓓ snow

2. The ___ is made up of nine planets and the Sun.

Ⓐ atmosphere
Ⓑ meteor
Ⓒ solar system
Ⓓ satellite

3. ___ is not part of the water cycle.

Ⓐ Evaporation
Ⓑ Weather
Ⓒ Condensation
Ⓓ Precipitation

4. ___ is not a flower part.

Ⓐ Sap Ⓒ Stamen
Ⓑ Pistil Ⓓ Petal

5. The food ___ shows the food groups for a balanced diet.

Ⓐ cycle Ⓒ pentagon
Ⓑ circle Ⓓ pyramid

6. While an animal hibernates,

Ⓐ its body gets warmer than usual.
Ⓑ it breathes more quickly.
Ⓒ its heart beats more slowly.
Ⓓ it eats lots of food.

7. Moving gas from a jar to a balloon would change

Ⓐ the shape of the gas.
Ⓑ the gas to liquid.
Ⓒ the color of the gas.
Ⓓ nothing.

8. A bar magnet would pick up pins

Ⓐ only at its north pole.
Ⓑ at all points equally.
Ⓒ mainly at its north and south poles.
Ⓓ only in its middle.

9. Current moves easily through

Ⓐ an insulator.
Ⓑ a conductor.
Ⓒ a charge.
Ⓓ an open switch.

Name ______________________ Date ____________

Earth and Space Science

Directions Darken the circle for the correct answer.

1. The breaking down and carrying away of soil is ___.
   Ⓐ moisture
   Ⓑ humidity
   Ⓒ erosion

2. The weight of the air pressing down on an area is ___.
   Ⓐ air pollution
   Ⓑ air conditioning
   Ⓒ air pressure

3. The liquid in a thermometer rises when the temperature ___.
   Ⓐ is cold
   Ⓑ is warm
   Ⓒ stays the same

4. The pull that keeps us on Earth is ___.
   Ⓐ gravity
   Ⓑ tides
   Ⓒ friction

5. The Moon moves in an orbit around ___.
   Ⓐ the Earth
   Ⓑ the Sun
   Ⓒ Saturn

6. In a solar eclipse, the Moon moves between ___ and the Sun.
   Ⓐ Venus
   Ⓑ the Earth
   Ⓒ the North Star

7. Air temperature, clouds, and rain are all part of Earth's ___.
   Ⓐ core
   Ⓑ erosion
   Ⓒ weather

8. Flat, gray clouds that bring rain are ___.
   Ⓐ stratus
   Ⓑ cumulus
   Ⓒ cirrus

9. Perspiration helps you feel cooler on hot days when the humidity is ___.
   Ⓐ high
   Ⓑ low
   Ⓒ the same

10. Petroleum that comes from the ground is ___.
    Ⓐ smog
    Ⓑ crude oil
    Ⓒ carbon dioxide

Name ______________________ Date ______________

Earth and Space Science, p. 2

Directions Answer each question in a complete sentence.

1. What does erosion do to the Earth's surface? ______________________

2. How do rivers form? ______________________

3. How does the Sun affect the weather? ______________________

4. What are some differences between hurricanes and tornadoes?

5. Why would a barometer have a lower reading on a mountaintop than at sea level? ______________________

Name ______________________ Date ____________

Life Science

Directions Darken the circle for the correct answer.

1. The green material in plants is
- Ⓐ pistil.
- Ⓑ money.
- Ⓒ chlorophyll.
- Ⓓ ink.

2. Plants without chlorophyll are
- Ⓐ spores.
- Ⓑ fungi.
- Ⓒ cones.
- Ⓓ trees.

3. To get sunlight, plants can turn their
- Ⓐ leaves.
- Ⓑ roots.
- Ⓒ stems.
- Ⓓ trunks.

4. Cereals, bread, and pasta are
- Ⓐ vegetables.
- Ⓑ fruits.
- Ⓒ meats.
- Ⓓ grains.

5. Calcium is an example of a
- Ⓐ mineral.
- Ⓑ protein.
- Ⓒ fat.
- Ⓓ carbohydrate.

6. Your heart beats faster when you
- Ⓐ run.
- Ⓑ sleep.
- Ⓒ read a book.
- Ⓓ watch television.

7. Features that living things have are called
- Ⓐ faces.
- Ⓑ groups.
- Ⓒ traits.
- Ⓓ backbones.

8. Flying south in winter is called
- Ⓐ hibernation.
- Ⓑ protection.
- Ⓒ digestion.
- Ⓓ migration.

9. Giving birth to live young and having fur are traits of
- Ⓐ birds.
- Ⓑ reptiles.
- Ⓒ amphibians.
- Ⓓ mammals.

10. All living things are made of
- Ⓐ walls.
- Ⓑ leaves.
- Ⓒ cells.
- Ⓓ organs.

Name ______________________ Date ____________

Life Science

Directions Label the parts of a flower.

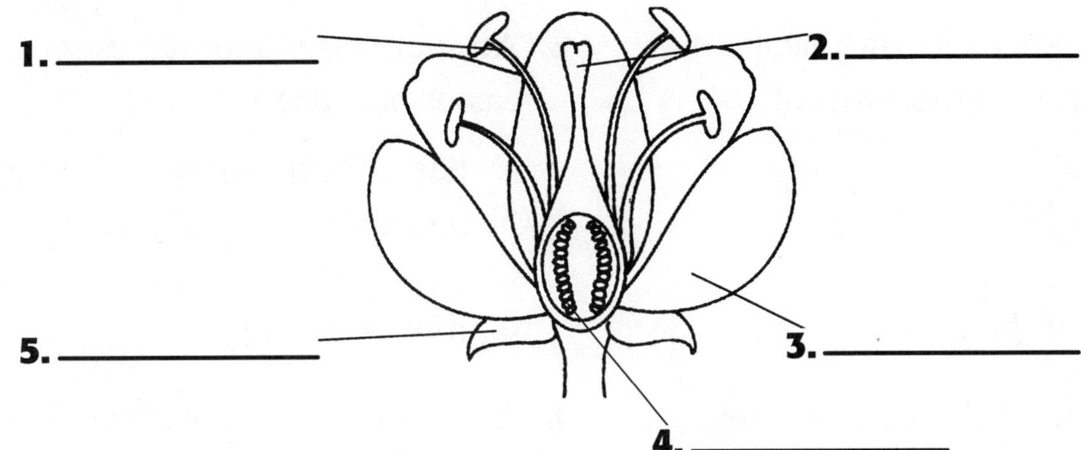

Directions Name the three things a plant needs to grow.

6. ______________________
7. ______________________
8. ______________________

Directions Name the other four animal groups. One is *amphibian*.

9. ______________________
10. ______________________
11. ______________________
12. ______________________

Directions Describe one adaptation that a snowshoe hare has that helps it survive.

13. ______________________

____

Name ______________________ Date ______________

Physical Science

Directions Darken the circle for the correct answer.

1. Matter keeps its own shape when it is in the form of

- Ⓐ a solid.
- Ⓑ a liquid.
- Ⓒ a gas.
- Ⓓ all of the above.

2. All of the following are the same form of matter except

- Ⓐ milk.
- Ⓑ lemon juice.
- Ⓒ oil.
- Ⓓ steam.

3. Sugar would dissolve most easily in water that is at

- Ⓐ 0° C.
- Ⓑ 18° C.
- Ⓒ 65° C.
- Ⓓ 100° C.

4. A magnet will pick up an object that is made of

- Ⓐ plastic.
- Ⓑ iron.
- Ⓒ wood.
- Ⓓ copper.

5. Work is done when

- Ⓐ a force is used.
- Ⓑ a force moves an object.
- Ⓒ nothing moves.
- Ⓓ a person holds something.

6. An inclined plane makes work easier because it

- Ⓐ has a sharp point.
- Ⓑ has a slanted surface.
- Ⓒ moves slowly.
- Ⓓ moves quickly.

7. All of these are machines that make work easier except a

- Ⓐ lever.
- Ⓑ pulley.
- Ⓒ spring scale.
- Ⓓ wedge.

8. The power in your arm that moves a paper airplane forward is

- Ⓐ lift.
- Ⓑ drag.
- Ⓒ thrust.
- Ⓓ gravity.

9. The source of electricity in a flashlight is the

- Ⓐ switch.
- Ⓑ metal.
- Ⓒ dry cell.
- Ⓓ bulb.

10. If a circuit is open,

- Ⓐ a light will go on.
- Ⓑ all the parts are connected.
- Ⓒ the switch may be off.
- Ⓓ a current will go through it.

Name ______________________ Date ____________

Physical Science

Directions Answer each question in complete sentences.

1. What is an example of matter changing from a liquid to a gas?

____

____

____

2. What are three things that a magnet can pick up?

____

____

____

3. What simple machine would you use to lift a bucket of water into a tree house 10 feet off the ground? Describe how it works.

____

____

____

4. What is a difference between an open and a closed electrical circuit?

____

____

____

5. On another sheet of paper, draw a new kind of flying machine that can do everything an airplane, a helicopter, and a rocket can do. Label the parts. What will your new flying machine do?

Science Portfolio Assessment

Student's Name ______________________________

Date ______________________________

Goals	Evidence and Comments
1. Growth in understanding science concepts	
2. Growth in using science processes	
3. Growth in thinking critically	
4. Growth in developing positive habits of mind and positive attitudes toward science	

Name ______________________ Date ______________

Social Studies Overall Assessment

Directions Darken the circle for the correct answer.

1. What does the *Constitution* describe?

Ⓐ how states can build highways and bridges
Ⓑ how the United States government works
Ⓒ how the city government provides services
Ⓓ how people show their patriotism

2. Why does each state need its own government?

Ⓐ Each state has its own problems to solve.
Ⓑ Some states have more people than other states.
Ⓒ States need to get taxes from the people.
Ⓓ All states need a state anthem.

3. Why are there 50 stars on the United States flag?

Ⓐ The stars stand for the Presidents of the United States.
Ⓑ One star is added to the flag every ten years.
Ⓒ The stars are for the heroes of the country.
Ⓓ There is one star for each state.

4. What are human resources?

Ⓐ raw materials
Ⓑ money used to make products
Ⓒ people who work for a company
Ⓓ marketing plans

5. The people who make products are

Ⓐ producers.
Ⓑ consumers.
Ⓒ users.
Ⓓ buyers.

Go on to the next page.

Name ______________________ Date ______________

Social Studies Overall Assessment, p. 2

Directions Darken the circle for the correct answer.

6. An *import* is a product that is

Ⓐ made for the first time.
Ⓑ sold to another country.
Ⓒ sold only in markets.
Ⓓ brought into a country from another country.

7. A community in which buying and selling goods is the main work is a

Ⓐ natural resource center.
Ⓑ capital city.
Ⓒ trading center.
Ⓓ county seat.

8. To manufacture something means to

Ⓐ grow it.
Ⓑ open it.
Ⓒ sell it.
Ⓓ make it.

9. The leader of a nation is called a

Ⓐ governor.
Ⓑ president.
Ⓒ mayor.
Ⓓ principal.

10. The way of life of a group of people is its

Ⓐ compass rose.
Ⓑ citizenship.
Ⓒ culture.
Ⓓ coastline.

Name ______________________ Date ____________

Social Studies Overall Assessment

Directions Write answers to each question in complete sentences.

1. What are three products you use every day?

____

____

____

2. What do *supply* and *demand* mean? Why do they go together?

____

____

____

____

3. What are the four points in a compass rose?

____

____

4. What is the difference between public property and private property? Give one example of each.

____

____

____

____

5. What are the names of the seven continents?

____

____

____

____

Name ______________________ Date ______________

Reading Maps

Directions Use the compass rose to answer the questions. Darken the circle for the correct answer to each question.

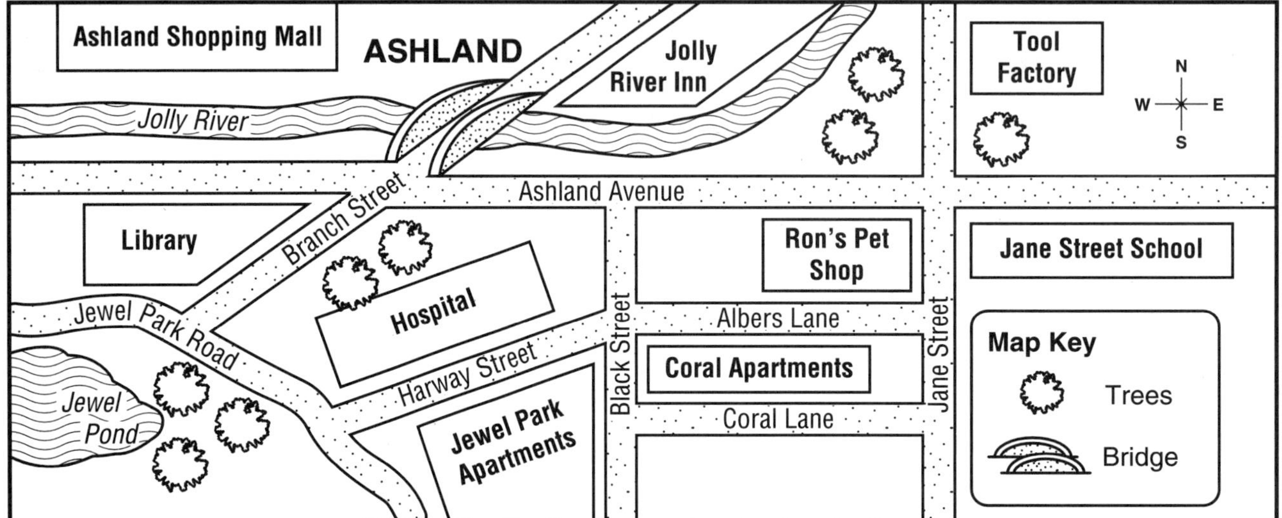

1. Which direction is the Ashland Shopping Mall from the Jane Street School?

Ⓐ northeast
Ⓑ northwest
Ⓒ southeast
Ⓓ southwest

2. If you walked from the library to the Jolly River Inn, in which direction would you walk?

Ⓐ northeast
Ⓑ northwest
Ⓒ southeast
Ⓓ southwest

3. In which direction would you walk to go from the library to the Jewel Park Apartments?

Ⓐ northeast
Ⓑ northwest
Ⓒ southeast
Ⓓ southwest

4. If you live in the Jewel Park Apartments and work at the Tool Factory, what direction is your home from your job?

Ⓐ northeast
Ⓑ northwest
Ⓒ southeast
Ⓓ southwest

Name ______________________ Date ____________

Reading Maps

Directions Study the symbols in the map key. Read and respond to the items below.

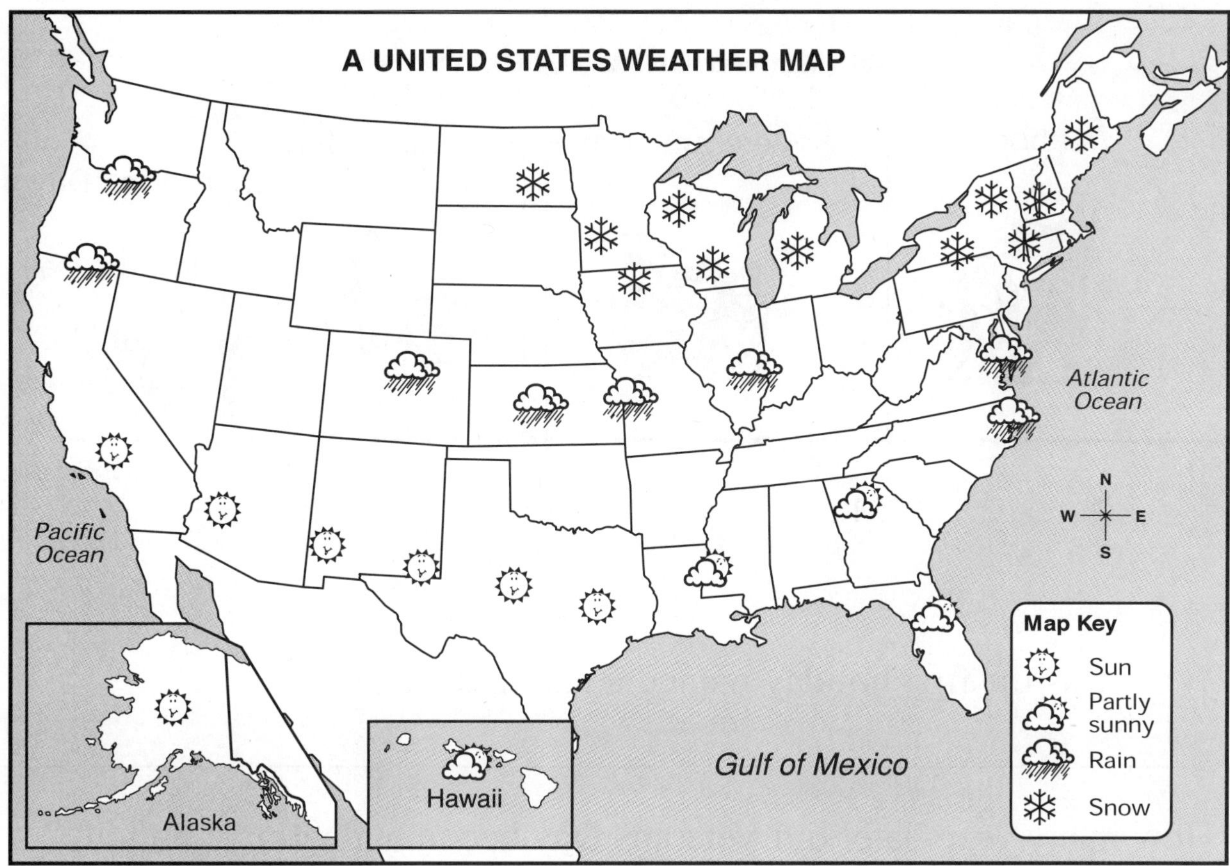

1. Circle the parts of the country where it is snowing.

2. Put an X on parts of the country where it is partly sunny.

3. Write the word *Rain* on the parts of the country where it is raining.

4. What is the weather in Hawaii? ______________________

Name ______________________ Date ____________

Reading Time Lines

Directions Use the time line about national holidays. Write answers to the questions.

SOME NATIONAL HOLIDAYS

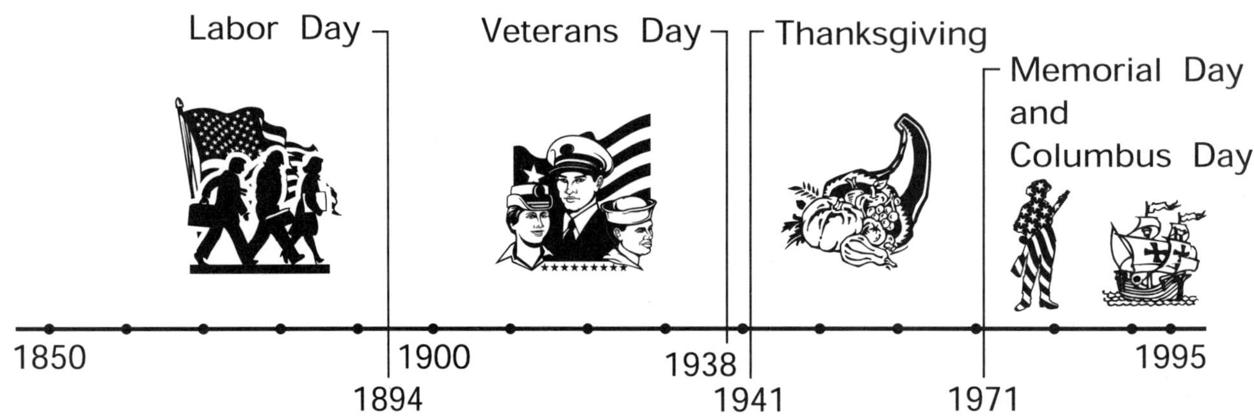

1. What was the first holiday named a national holiday?

____

2. How many years later did Veterans Day become a national holiday?

____

3. What celebration became a national holiday in 1941?

____

4. Was Veterans Day made a national holiday before or after Thanksgiving?

____

Skills Assessments, Grade 3
Answer Key

Page 5
1. tiger, **2.** star, **3.** five, **4.** B, **5.** C, **6.** A, **7.** C, **8.** D
Page 6
9. A, **10.** C, **11.** C, **12.** D, **13.** Answers will vary. Kate hit the ball and at least one runner scored.
Page 7
1. v, **2.** f, **3.** k, **4.** c, **5.** p, **6.** b, **7.** d, **8.** n, **9.** x, **10.** t, **11.** b, **12.** r, **13.** m, **14.** l, **15.** s, **16.** g
Page 8
1. D, **2.** D, **3.** A, **4.** C, **5.** B, **6.** B, **7.** A., **8.** D, **9.** B, **10.** D
Page 9
1. u, **2.** o, **3.** i, **4.** o, **5.** a, **6.** e, **7.** i, **8.** a, **9.** e, **10.** a, **11.** o, **12.** u, **13.** a, **14.** y, **15.** e, **16.** i
Page 10
1. farm, **2.** dirt, **3.** cart, **4.** horses, **5.** herd, **6.** hurt, **7.** nurse, **8.** porch
Page 11
1. B, **2.** A, **3.** B, **4.** B, **5.** A, **6.** B, **7.** B, **8.** C, **9.** B, **10.** A
Page 12
1. D, **2.** A, **3.** D, **4.** C, **5.** B, **6.** D, **7.** B, **8.** C, **9.** B, **10.** B
Page 13
1. A, **2.** C, **3.** B, **4.** C, **5.** A, **6.** C, **7.** D, **8.** C, **9.** A, **10.** C
Page 14
1. C, **2.** D, **3.** C, **4.** A, **5.** D, **6.** B, **7.** C, **8.** D, **9.** B, **10.** A
Page 15
1. A, **2.** D, **3.** A, **4.** C, **5.** C, **6.** A, **7.** C, **8.** B, **9.** B, **10.** A
Page 16
1. C, **2.** A, **3.** A, **4.** B, **5.** D, **6.** B, **7.** A, **8.** D, **9.** C, **10.** D
Page 17
1. egg, **2.** duck, **3.** hive, **4.** kitten, **5.** cold, **6.** uncle, **7.** thin, **8.** birds, **9.** horns, **10.** fur
Page 18
1. C, **2.** A, **3.** D, **4.** B, **5.** C, **6.** A, **7.** B, **8.** D, **9.** C, **10.** B
Page 19
1. B, **2.** C, **3.** B, **4.** B, **5.** A, **6.** B
Page 20
1. C, **2.** A, **3.** B, **4.** A, **5.** D, **6.** B
Page 21
1. B, **2.** A, **3.** B, **4.** C
Page 22
1. A, **2.** B, **3.** D, **4.** A
Page 23
1. C, **2.** A, **3.** A
Page 24
1. A, **2.** A, **3.** A
Page 26
1. B, **2.** A, **3.** D, **4.** A, **5.** B
Page 28
Answers will vary. **1.** A little bird was on the windowsill. **2.** The cage had a swing, a mirror, a bell, water, food, and treats. **3.** The people left the window and the cage door open. **4.** He couldn't find food, and he didn't like to eat worms and bugs. **5.** He felt trapped.
Page 30
1. B, **2.** B, **3.** C, **4.** D, **5.** A
Page 32
Answers will vary. **1.** The candlemaker was from Brighton. **2.** He enjoyed making them so much that he didn't ask people to pay for them. **3.** He used dye, tallow, and string. **4.** They didn't have any other lights. **5.** Answers will vary. Accept reasonable responses supported by evidence from the story.
Page 34
1. B, **2.** D, **3.** C, **4.** A, **5.** C
Page 36
1. Answers will vary. Any of the following are correct: temperature, water, wind, air pressure, clouds, and sunshine. **2.** A tropical storm becomes a hurricane when its winds reach 75 miles per hour.
3. A hurricane causes so much damage because its winds can reach 150 miles per hour, it has very heavy rains, and it can last 14 days.
4. A tornado forms when warm air meets cold air and the atmosphere becomes unstable. A funnel of high wind forms.
5. A tornado over the ocean is called a waterspout. A tornado over the desert is called a sand devil.
Page 37
1. D, **2.** C, **3.** B, **4.** E, **5.** D, **6.** B, **7.** A, **8.** B, **9.** D, **10.** A
Page 38
1. d, **2.** e, **3.** a, **4.** b, **5.** f, **6.** c, **7.** i, **8.** k, **9.** l, **10.** j, **11.** h, **12.** g, **13.** stand, stone, tall, test
Page 39
1. A, **2.** B, **3.** C, **4.** E, **5.** D, **6.** B, **7.** D, **8.** B, **9.** B, **10.** D
Page 40
1. B, **2.** C, **3.** A, **4.** A, **5.** D, **6.** C, **7.** A, **8.** A, **9.** B, **10.** A
Page 41
1. D, **2.** C, **3.** A, **4.** B, **5.** A, **6.** D, **7.** E, **8.** C, **9.** E, **10.** D
Page 42
1. C, **2.** D, **3.** A, **4.** B, **5.** C, **6.** C, **7.** D, **8.** A, **9.** C, **10.** B
Page 43
1. A, **2.** B, **3.** D, **4.** B, **5.** C, **6.** C, **7.** B, **8.** B, **9.** D, **10.** A
Page 44
1. D, **2.** D, **3.** A, **4.** D, **5.** C, **6.** B, **7.** B, **8.** A, **9.** D, **10.** D
Page 45
1. B, **2.** D, **3.** B, **4.** C, **5.** A, **6.** D, **7.** B, **8.** A, **9.** C, **10.** A
Page 46
1. B, **2.** B, **3.** C, **4.** A, **5.** C, **6.** A, **7.** C, **8.** B, **9.** A, **10.** C
Page 47
1. B, **2.** A, **3.** A, **4.** B, **5.** B, **6.** B, **7.** C, **8.** B, **9.** C, **10.** C
Page 48
1. B, **2.** C, **3.** D, **4.** B, **5.** B, **6.** C
Page 49
1. A, **2.** D, **3.** A, **4.** C, **5.** C, **6.** D, **7.** C, **8.** D, **9.** A, **10.** C
Page 50
1. C, **2.** A, **3.** C, **4.** D, **5.** C, **6.** A, **7.** B, **8.** B, **9.** B, **10.** C
Page 52
1. B, **2.** B, **3.** A, **4.** D, **5.** C, **6.** A, **7.** C, **8.** B, **9.** B
Page 53
1. ART PROJECTS AT THE BEACH; **2.** Sandy Shore; **3.** Crafts Books, Inc.; **4.** Getting Started; **5.** pages 8-10, page 26, page 29; **6.** page 32; **7.** page 8, pages 10-30; **8.** 8 pages; **9.** table of contents; **10.** table of contents, index
Page 54
1. aardvark, **2.** bat, **3.** deer, **4.** frog, **5.** horse, **6.** monkey, **7.** panda, **8.** snake, **9.** tiger, **10.** zebra, **11.** stamp/track, **12.** track, **13.** stamp, track, **14.** marks left by a person, an animal, or a thing, **15.** verb
Page 55
1. C, **2.** A, **3.** D, **4.** C, **5.** B, **6.** A
Page 56
1. middle, **2.** beginning, **3.** ending, **4.** Animal tracks can tell you many things. **5.** Answers will vary. Be sure that details refer to main idea. **6.** Answers will vary. Be sure that the paragraph has a main idea and details that support the main idea.
Page 57
1. Rosa wants to thank her aunt for the shirt. **2.** October 8, 2001. We know because of the date. **3.** Rosa wrote the letter. We know because of the signature. **4.** Answers will vary. A friendly letter has a heading, a greeting, a body, a closing, and a signature.

Answer Key, p. 2

Page 58
1. This how-to paragraph teaches how to tie-dye a shirt. **2.** Answers may vary. Examples include start, next, then, and finally. **3.** Finally, remove all the rubber bands to see your brightly colored, tie-dyed shirt. **4.** Answers will vary. A how-to paragraph has a topic sentence, has detail sentences that tell what materials are needed, uses time order words, and gives directions in order.

Page 59
1. Casey would not wear green pants. **2.** Lori made the pants fit Casey by cutting a hole for Casey's tail. **3.** Casey has a tail, and Casey said "Meow." **4.** Answers will vary. A descriptive paragraph tells what someone or something is like and paints a vivid and clear word-picture.

Page 60
1. The best building material for a house is brick. **2.** Answers will vary. Possible responses: A brick house stays cool in summer and warm in winter. Bricks never need to be painted. A brick house will keep people dry. A wolf cannot blow down a house made of bricks. **3.** A wolf cannot blow down a house made of bricks. **4.** Answers will vary. A persuasive paragraph tells the writer's feelings, lists reasons, and asks readers to agree with the writer.

Page 61
1. C, **2.** A, **3.** C, **4.** C, **5.** C, **6.** B, **7.** A, **8.** A, **9.** D, **10.** B

Page 62
1. =, **2.** <, **3.** >, **4.** 1,550; 1,604; 1,605; 1,649; 1,650, **5.** 500, **6.** 6, **7.** 1,230, **8.** triangle, **9.** $1.25, **10.** 8, **11.** Answers will vary. Response should include a summer activity. **12.** both hands pointing to the "3" on the clock face

Page 63
1. B, **2.** D, **3.** A, **4.** B, **5.** A, **6.** B, **7.** D, **8.** C

Page 64
1. E, **2.** B, **3.** A, **4.** C, **5.** D, **6.** <, **7.** <, **8.** >, **9.** =, **10.** >, **11.** =, **12.** 15, **13.** 150, **14.** 1,500, answers to 15-17 can be in any order: **15.** 3+7=10; **16.** 10-7=3; **17.** 10-3=7

Page 65
1. A, **2.** C, **3.** A, **4.** B, **5.** A, **6.** C, **7.** B, **8.** C, **9.** D, **10.** C

Page 66
1. D, **2.** B, **3.** A, **4.** A, **5.** C, **6.** B, **7.** A, **8.** D, **9.** A, **10.** C

Page 67
1. D, **2.** C, **3.** B, **4.** C, **5.** A, **6.** C, **7.** A, **8.** B, **9.** A, **10.** A

Page 68
1. C, **2.** D, **3.** B, **4.** C, **5.** 6 faces; 12 edges; 8 vertices; **6.** 1 face; 0 edges; 0 vertices

Page 69
1. A, **2.** B, **3.** D, **4.** B, **5.** A, **6.** D, **7.** B, **8.** B, **9.** B, **10.** C

Page 70
1. B, **2.** C, **3.** B, **4.** B, **5.** D, **6.** B, **7.** D, **8.** A

Page 71
1. Basketball, **2.** 24, **3.** 42, **4.** Answers will vary. Check to see if answer matches survey results. **5.** B, **6.** A, **7.** C, **8.** B

Page 72
1. B, **2.** D, **3.** C, **4.** A, **5.** C, **6.** A, **7.** D, **8.** C, **9.** A, **10.** D

Page 73
1. 15 dots in same configuration; **2.** 16 dots (4x4), 25 dots (5x5); **3.** 4x2 dots, 5x2 dots, 6x2 dots; **4.** 11 dots; **5.** 11 dots

Page 74
1. $1.17, **2.** $6.12, **3.** a, **4.** c, **5.** Answers will vary. Coins must equal 58¢. **6.** Answers will vary. Coins and bills must equal $2.53. **7.** 1 half dollar and 2 pennies **8.** 1 quarter, 1 dime, 1 nickel, 1 penny

Page 75
1. 11:00, **2.** 5:20, **3.** 3:50, **4.** 8:22, **5.** 9:55, **6.** 4:00, **7.** D, **8.** C

Page 76
1. A, **2.** C, **3.** B, **4.** A, **5.** D, **6.** A, **7.** B, **8.** D, **9.** 1 inch, **10.** 5 centimeters

Page 77
1. A, **2.** B, **3.** C, **4.** A, **5.** B, **6.** D, **7.** C

Page 78
1. 9, **2.** 39° F, **3.** 20 years old, **4.** Ethan, **5.** 16 pounds, **6.** Answers may vary. Examples include 461, 614, 641, 560, and 605. **7.** $16.00, **8.** 21 coloring books

Page 79
1. A, **2.** D, **3.** A, **4.** 89¢, **5.** 71° F, **6.** more

Page 80
1. B, **2.** C, **3.** A, **4.** D, **5.** B, **6.** D, **7.** A, **8.** C

Page 81
1. A, **2.** C, **3.** B, **4.** A, **5.** D, **6.** C, **7.** A, **8.** C, **9.** B

Page 82
1. C, **2.** C, **3.** B, **4.** A, **5.** A, **6.** B, **7.** C, **8.** A, **9.** B, **10.** B

Page 83
Answers will vary. **1.** Erosion carries away soil so no plants can grow. **2.** Rivers form when melting snow or rain runs down the mountain. As it gains speed, it carves out a channel and carries bits of rock and dirt with it. Then it becomes a stream. When several streams join together, it becomes a river. **3.** It heats up the Earth in some regions more than others. The equator has warm, mild temperatures, while the poles are cold and frigid. **4.** Hurricanes are larger and last for many days, cover a greater area, and form over the ocean. **5.** Air pressure is less at higher levels because there is less air above pressing down.

Page 84
1. C, **2.** B, **3.** A, **4.** D, **5.** A, **6.** A, **7.** C, **8.** D, **9.** D, **10.** C

Page 85
clockwise from top left: **1.** stamen **2.** pistil **3.** petal **4.** ovules **5.** sepal **6.-8.** oxygen, water, light **9.-12.** fish, reptiles, birds, mammals **13.** Answers will vary. Body covering changes color seasonally to camouflage it from predators. Big feet do not sink into snow. Fur protects if from the cold.

Page 86
1. A, **2.** D, **3.** D, **4.** B, **5.** B, **6.** B, **7.** C, **8.** C, **9.** C, **10.** C

Page 87
Answers will vary. **1.** When water is boiled, it changes into water vapor. **2.** Magnets pick up metal material. Examples include paper clips, nails, some keys. **3.** You would use a pulley to lift a bucket of water into a treehouse 10 feet off of the ground. A pulley is a wheel with a rope wrapped around it. One end of the rope is tied to the bucket of water, and the other end is pulled by a person. **4.** In a closed circuit, all parts of the circuit have been joined, and the circuit works. In an open circuit, at least one part is not joined. **5.** Responses should describe the features drawn.

Page 89
1. B, **2.** A, **3.** D, **4.** C, **5.** A

Page 90
6. D, **7.** C, **8.** D, **9.** B, **10.** C

Page 91
Answers will vary. **1.** Possible answers are food, clothing, and cars. **2.** Supply is the amount of products or services that is ready for sale. Demand is the amount of products or services that people want to buy. Supply and demand are both about products and services. **3.** The four points on a compass rose are north, east, south, west. **4.** Public property belongs to all the people. Examples include a city hall, a park, and a library. Private property belongs to one person or a group of people. Examples include a house, a grocery store, and a shopping mall. **5.** North America, South America, Africa, Asia, Europe, Australia, Antarctica.

Page 92
1. B, **2.** A, **3.** C, **4.** D

Page 93
1. States with the snow symbol should be circled. **2.** States with the partly sunny symbol should have an X on them. **3.** States that have a rain symbol should have *Rain* written on them. **4.** partly sunny

Page 94
1. Labor Day, **2.** 44 years later, **3.** Thanksgiving, **4.** before